Counter

*Berkley Books by Tripp Evans
and Andrew Frothingham*

WAKE UP AND SMELL THE COFFEE

...and by Andrew Frothingham

HOW TO MAKE USE OF A USELESS DEGREE

Most Berkley Books are available at special quantity discounts for bulk purchases for sales promotions, premiums, fund-raising or educational use. Special books, or book excerpts, can also be created to fit specific needs.

For details, write to Special Markets, The Berkley Publishing Group, 200 Madison Avenue, New York, New York 10016.

The S-Factor Stress Gram Counter

*Rating Life's Hardships—
the Easy Way!*

Andrew Frothingham, Ed.M.,
& Tripp Evans, M.S.W.

BERKLEY BOOKS, NEW YORK

This book is an original publication of The Berkley Publishing Group.

THE S-FACTOR STRESS GRAM COUNTER

A Berkley Book / published by arrangement with the authors

PRINTING HISTORY
Berkley trade paperback edition / April 1998

All rights reserved.
Copyright © 1998 by Andrew Frothingham and Tripp Evans.
Text design by Irving Perkins Associates.
This book may not be reproduced in whole or in part,
by mimeograph or any other means, without permission.
For information address: The Berkley Publishing Group,
a member of Penguin Putnam Inc.,
200 Madison Avenue, New York, New York 10016.

The Penguin Putnam Inc. World Wide Web site address is
http://www.penguinputnam.com

ISBN: 0-425-16159-5

BERKLEY®
Berkley Books are published by The Berkley Publishing
Group, a member of Penguin Putnam Inc.,
200 Madison Avenue, New York, New York 10016.
BERKLEY and the "B" design
are trademarks belonging to Berkley Publishing Corporation.

PRINTED IN THE UNITED STATES OF AMERICA
10 9 8 7 6 5 4 3 2 1

This book is dedicated to our absolute favorite stressors—Morgan, Luke and Evan.

Introduction

Stress is all around us; it's part of our daily experience from the moment we wake up in the morning until we go to bed at night. Running late for work? Stress. Troubles with your loved one? Stress. Can't decide what to have for dinner? Stress. Difficulty sleeping? Stress. Stub your toe? Stress. Stress kicks in when we're hurt, cornered, powerless, confused, anxious, overwhelmed, helpless, shocked, confronted, surprised, in danger, frustrated or just pissed off.

What Happens When You're Under Stress?

Stress accelerates the heart rate, increases perspiration to cool the skin down and releases endorphins to relieve pain. In other words, when you're under stress, you sweat like a pig, pant like a dog and act crazy as a loon. Believe it or not, stress isn't always a bad thing. Adrenaline, part of the stress response, gives athletes the extra energy needed to perform in competition. Stress-induced adrenaline gives parents strength to perform those superhuman feats we see on TV, like lifting a two-ton car off their baby. We all experience this biochemical event. It's akin to taking LSD, Prozac, amphetamines or three-hour-old diner coffee.

A traffic jam (12.53) is a perfect example of a stress-inducing event: you are powerless and angry. Your adrenaline is up. You want to do something but you're stuck. Sure, you can sit on your horn, open your window and shout at the car ahead of you, or whip out the car phone and abuse someone on talk radio, but nothing's going to change the fact that Route 687 is still one big parking lot.

So What Can You Do About It?

Well, nothing really. And since you can't do anything about it, why not get some credit for it? But how can one possibly compare sitting in the middle of a traffic jam with, let's say, burping in front of your boss (9.272) or having to refold a map (64.78)? That's where this book comes in. After hours of exhaustive research (34.602), we've successfully and arbitrarily come up with the ultimate in stress scales: The S-Factor Stress Gram Counter. (That's what all those numbers in parentheses are.)

The S-Factor Stress Gram Counter vs. Those Other Scales

We took the stress ratings out of Psychology 101 textbooks and magazines we found on supermarket check-out racks and expanded the hell out of them. Their scales were boring, short and woefully incomplete. Instead of thirty or forty grossly general topics (e.g., vacation—13), we've fine-tuned the list with many more complete entries of our own (e.g., vacation with kids—31.044, vacation with kids and the family pet—38.94, going on vacation and it rains all damn week—41.33). The range of their scale goes from a simple 1 to 100. The higher the number, the more stressful the situation. Ours goes from .007 (watching a James Bond movie) to 151 (your ex shows up drunk at your wedding). As you may have noticed, we've included numbers to the right of the decimal point to help make your score even more precise. For example, death of first parent, if you never said "I love you," is 103.756, while death of a salesman is .03.

Look at the list, find the specific stress that relates to your situation and check out its corresponding number. Voilà! That's the S-Factor Stress Gram value. This number system makes it easy to compare completely different stress situations. For example, dealing with a boss is 20.64, attending a tenth high school reunion is 20.003 and having your luggage be the last to come off the conveyor at the airport is 20.3. Therefore, it's easy to determine that coping with your boss is ever so slightly (0.637 and 0.34 respectively) higher than the other two.

We Can Get Stressed Out Too, You Know

While we tried to be comprehensive and include every imaginable stressor, we got stressed (67.02) and probably missed a few. For this reason, we've left some blank pages for you to write in your own stressors. In order to assign an appropriate S-Factor Stress Gram value, all you need to do is familiarize yourself with the situations we present and come up with a number that's close. Get at least two friends to agree and it's law. Pretty unstressful, huh?

The S-Factor Stress Gram Counter

S-Factor Stress Gram Values

ABORT	25.54
ACCESS DENIED	31.8
AGING	
Being asked who's younger, you or a much older sibling	4.653
Being asked who's younger, you or one of your parents	15.78
Being called Sir or Madam for the first time	13.711
Being stopped by a cop young enough to be your child	18.050
Discovering that most commercials are aimed at people much younger than you are	4.765
Discovering the first gray hair (over 30)	32.23

Discovering the first gray hair (under 30)	43.56
Discovering a gray hair if found on body part other than head	20.69
Discovering the first gray hair on your spouse's jacket	44.7
Discovering the rock station you're listening to is really the easy-listening station	15.85
Forgetting a frequently called phone number	5.55
Forgetting an appointment with a business associate	26.77
Forgetting an appointment with a friend	6.77
Forgetting an appointment with your shrink	87.9
Getting a hearing aid and hearing what they're saying about you: if it's positive	5.908
Getting a hearing aid and hearing what they're saying about you: if it's negative	59.08
Getting age spots on the back of your hands	3.22

The S-Factor Stress Gram Counter

Getting false teeth	12.88
Getting false teeth, and being served corn on the cob	18.4
Getting false teeth, and they develop cavities	47.91
Having a clerk automatically give you a Senior Citizen's discount	10.85
Having to give up spicy foods	3.057
Having to wear glasses to read this book	???
HAVING TO WEAR GLASSES TO READ THIS BOOK	20.10
Looking in the mirror and seeing one of your parents staring back	10.64
Looking in the mirror and seeing one of your grandparents staring back	20.9
Losing 40% of your hearing	???
LOSING 40% OF YOUR HEARING!!	52.118
Not knowing Nine Inch Nails' latest lyrics	1.9
Not knowing Nine Inch Nails is a rock band	12.93
Realizing that the President is younger than you	8.224

Realizing that the TV stars you think are sexy are young enough to be your children	9.021
Realizing that you've fallen and can't get up	1-800
Realizing you sound like one of your parents	15.981
Realizing you think like one of your parents	26.761
Realizing you value sleep as much as sex	18.669
Walking down the street on a stormy day, coming to a stop sign and getting ready to cross when some kid dressed up in a Boy Scout uniform taps you on the shoulder and asks if he can help you across and you get really pissed and you give him the finger and the little twerp starts to cry and somebody sees what's going on and starts yelling at you and it causes a scene and a crowd of people gather and start calling you names like "dirty old pervert" or "child abuser"	51.21

Starting to calculate the years left

before you qualify for a senior citizen discount	3.265
Starting to calculate the years you could have been using your senior citizen discount	3.265
Starting to drive sensibly to set a good example for the kids	2.655
The impact of the onset of Alzheimer's	46.442
The impact of the onset of Alzheimer's	46.442
The impact of the onset of Alzheimer's	46.442
The impact of full-blown Alzheimer's	0
Becoming incontinent at 40	69.922
Becoming incontinent at 50	59.23
Becoming incontinent at 60	49.65
Becoming incontinent at 80	4.6
Becoming incontinent when you have an orgasm	87
Adult diapers—wearing them	52.954
Starting to find the Depends commercial interesting	13.030

AMBULANCE DRIVER

Driving an ambulance	37.9
Driving an ambulance in Lebanon	97.3

AMERICAN INDIAN

Being an American Indian in a land stolen from you	59
Being an American Indian who owns part of a casino	9.99

ANNIVERSARY

Remembering an anniversary the day of the anniversary	48.93
Forgetting a wedding anniversary	54.9
Your spouse forgets your wedding anniversary	6.83
Anniversary of the death of a pet	20.832
Anniversary of date of retirement	22.92
Anniversary of a failed marriage	36.8
Anniversary of the death of a parent	38.9
Anniversary of the last time you had sex with someone other than yourself	19.08

Looking for that special anniversary gift but not giving yourself enough time and your spouse knows you well enough to bet that you'll probably end up getting something stupid like another bunch of flowers so you make some quick calls to his or her friends

and ask if they have any suggestions but they're no help except for one who has the perfect idea but there's no way you can get it in time because it has to be special ordered and your anniversary is tomorrow	20.63
First anniversary of the last win by the local professional sports franchise	7.84
Second anniversary of the last win by the local professional sports franchise	9.84
Third anniversary of the last win by the local professional sports franchise	11.29
Tenth anniversary of the last win by the local professional sports franchise	19.99
Twentieth anniversary of the last win by the local professional sports franchise	16.42
Anniversary of your town losing its local professional sports franchise	27.85

ARGUMENT

Argument with a client	50.7
Argument with a client who owes you money	55.016
Argument with a coworker	30.52

Argument with a lover, when you know you're right	8
Argument with a lover, when you know you're wrong	38.8
Argument with a lover, when you know you're in public	42.7
Argument with a spouse, in front of your coworkers	30.352
Argument with a spouse, in front of your friends	27.95
Argument with a spouse, in front of the children	25.8
Argument with a spouse, in front of your in-laws	22.8
Argument with a spouse, in front of your parents	11.8
Argument with a spouse, in front of your cat	4.87
Argument with a spouse, when you've had the same argument before	19.642
Argument with your boss	35.97
Argument with a business partner	22.8
Argument with a parent	38.931
Argument with a police officer	40.9

Argument with a shouter	50.854
Argument with a stepchild	51
Argument with a 3-year-old who's right	60.865
Argument with an engineer	8.9
Argument with an evangelist	10.8
Argument with an ex-con	44.8
Argument with an ex-con who served time for murder	64.8
Argument with an ex-spouse	64.8
Argument with an in-law	21.23
Argument with someone else's child	2.76
Argument with your child	27.6
Argument with your Siamese twin	50.50

ASKING

Asking a date if they've been tested for AIDS	72.8
Asking a potential lover to use a condom	14.21
Asking a smoker to put his/her butt out	9.59
Asking for a raise from a nice boss	27.465
Asking for a raise from a mean boss	47.465

Asking for directions (female)	1.1
Asking for directions (male)	39.999
Asking for spare change when you're broke	16.6
Asking someone for a date	30.28
Asking someone in the next stall to lend you some toilet paper	49.23
Asking someone to dance	7.8
Asking where your glasses are when you are wearing them	20.20
Asking who wrote the book of love	5.5
Asking your kids if they take drugs	59.4

BABY

Accidentally hitting your baby on the soft spot on the top of the head	49.53
Accidentally leaving your baby in a restaurant	68.32
Accidentally leaving your baby on the roof of the car	88.82
Leaving the kid with the baby-sitter for the first time	39.4
Not being able to get a baby-sitter	37.38

Paying the baby-sitter more than you make	27.9
BABY-SITTING	
Baby-sitting for a child possessed by Satan	66.6
Baby-sitting for a child with the flu	66.6
Baby-sitting for a hyperactive child	66.7
Baby-sitting for a family that doesn't have cable	49.23
Baby-sitting for a family that doesn't have TV	54.19
Baby-sitting for a family that has only health food in the refrigerator	63.9
Baby-sitting for parents that call in to check every hour	22
Baby-sitting for twins	22.222
Baby-sitting for triplets	33.333
BALD	
Going bald before you hit 21 (male)	38.9
Going bald before you hit 21 (female)	93.8
BAT	
Having a live bat in the house	13.52

BATHROOM—PRISON

Having to use a bucket in a prison cell	8.98
Having to use a bucket in a prison cell, with the guard watching	15.34
Having to use a bucket in a prison cell, with your cellmate watching	17.554
Having to use a bucket in a prison cell, on orders from your cellmate	27.4

BATHROOM—PRIVATE

Cleaning the bathroom	94.281
Discovering the toilet seat is up after you have sat down	15.8
Finally getting to the bathroom and nothing comes out	18.33
Getting a phone call while on the toilet	14.14
Having the toilet bowl overflow	37.3
Having the toilet clog up after you pee	11.1
Having the toilet clog up after you poop	22.2
Living with someone who squeezes the toothpaste tube in the middle	13.886
Living with someone who cares if you squeeze the toothpaste tube in the middle	17.86

The S-Factor Stress Gram Counter 15

Using the Preparation H instead of the toothpaste	53.886
BATHROOM—PUBLIC	
Accidentally dropping your wedding ring into a clean toilet bowl	4.876
Accidentally dropping your wedding ring into a backed-up toilet bowl	48.3
Being in the bathroom when someone explodes the plumbing system	M-80
Having no reading material in the bathroom	9.42
Reading a mystery in the bathroom and finding the last two chapters torn out	11.89
Having someone sit in the stall next to yours when all the others are vacant	18.33
Having the toilet not flush completely	7.33
Having to give a urine sample for a test and nothing comes out	29.22
Having to use a hole in the ground in a Third World country	11.73
Having to use an army bathroom with no stalls for the first time	19.4

Having to use leaves for toilet paper while camping	12.53
Having to use leaves for toilet paper while camping and having those leaves turn out to be poison ivy	25.632
Leaving the bathroom unzipped	2.9
Leaving the bathroom unzipped and being told by a stranger	5.9
Leaving the bathroom unzipped and being told by a date	12.9
Looking down into a toilet you are using and seeing a rat coming up the drain	18.33
Looking down into a toilet you are using and seeing a snake coming up the drain	16.8
Looking up from a toilet you are using and seeing a security camera pointed your way	34.77
No lock on the bathroom stall door	6.33
No mirror	2.32
No stall door	13.864
No toilet paper	15.62
Peeing in the ocean	1.66

Peeing in the ocean and attracting a school of hungry fish	65
Peeing in the pool	5.84
Peeing in the pool and getting caught	70.02
Sitting down and discovering someone has pissed on the seat	25.52
Sitting down and the building fire alarm goes off	27.442
Taking a crap and having your shirttail get wet	21.77
Taking a leak while all dressed up and hitting your tie	22.77
Taps that automatically turn themselves off	15.888
The last person before you didn't flush	7.33
The last 12 people before you didn't flush	37.64
The person before you did flush and it flowed over	17.821
Those damn hot air blowers	66.8
Washing your hands in a public bathroom and accidentally spraying water on your crotch area	41.886

BED

Discovering you've slept through the alarm	57.984
Getting up on a workday	41.5
Getting up on a weekend	2.65
Going to bed late at night when you know you have to wake up early	19.33
Having a secret and knowing you talk in your sleep	29.312
Putting the kids (age 0 to 5) to bed	25.821
Putting the kids (age 6 to 15) to bed	27.33
Putting the kids (age 16 to 20) to bed	11.82
Putting the kids (age 21 to 30) to bed	5.77
Putting the kids (age 31 to 40) to bed	.88
Sleeping next to a snorer	13.6
Sleeping next to a tooth grinder	9.43
Sleeping on a pullout couch	8.2
Sleeping on the wet spot	16.112
Sleeping with a sheet hog	11.6

BEING AN ACTOR

Being called a thespian	4.31
After 29 years of work, being called an overnight success	36.7

After 29 years of work, still being unknown	74.997
Being a stuntperson in a James Bond movie	54.8
Being a stuntperson in a Merchant-Ivory movie	3.9
Getting second billing after an animal	58.686
Sharing the stage with a child	62.7

BIKING

Biking and hearing a car door start to open directly in front of you	36.33
Biking and slipping forward off the seat (if you're female)	20.55
Biking and slipping forward off the seat (if you're male)	93
Biking in freezing rain	28.28
Biking in New York City	56.33
Biking as a messenger in Boston	40.443
Biking on the L.A. Freeway	49.99
Biking through a dog-filled neighborhood	39.111
Biking up a San Francisco hill	61.82

Biking when your bike seat is too small	16.2
Biking with a broken leg	51.92
Getting a flat tire in the middle of a bike trip without a repair kit	62.11

BIRDS

Being target bombed by a pigeon while you're wearing a new hat	23.908
Being target bombed by a pigeon while you're not wearing a hat	26.908
The pet shop sells you a dead parrot, and denies it	39.2
Your parrot was taught to talk by a sailor	62.55

BIRTH

Giving birth to triplets when you thought you were only having one child	77.7
Giving birth with drugs	2.921
Giving birth without drugs because you want to	38.2
Giving birth without drugs because you're afraid of your Lamaze teacher	41.9
Having to watch the video of a birth	20.645

Postpartum depression (the father)	6.431
Postpartum depression (the mother)	51.22

BIRTHDAY

Having a Leap Year birthday	2.29
Having to give a birthday party for a 5-year-old	49.88
No one remembers your birthday and you're a child	74.3
No one remembers your birthday and you're an adult	24.3
No one remembers your birthday and you're old	4.3
Willard Scott announces your 100th birthday when you are only 89	41.3
Your birthday is December 25	12.25

BLADDER PROBLEMS

Having to go ten minutes after you just went	32.94
Having to go to the bathroom and there's none around	11.78
Having to go to the bathroom and having your spouse, who's driving, tell you to hold it for three more exits	31.111

Having to go to the bathroom in the middle of a traffic jam	15.632
Having to go to the bathroom in the middle of a subtitled, slow-moving, romantic movie	3.12
Having to go to the bathroom in the middle of a fast-paced, pyrotechnic, high-body-count, action-packed movie	31.2
Having to go to the bathroom in the middle of a business meeting	9.3
Having to interrupt someone pouring his/her heart out to you to go to the bathroom	6.381

BLINDNESS

Being blind from an accident	88.251
Being blind from birth	31.5
Trying not to use the words "look" or "see" when talking to a blind person	20.20
Being blind and having people get all embarrassed when they use the words "look" or "see" when talking to you	6.77
Losing your car license because of progressive blindness	53.33

The S-Factor Stress Gram Counter

BODY

Being flat-chested (female)	32A
Being flat-chested (male)	1.87
Having love handles (male)	7.54
Having saddlebags (female)	15.978
Having the body of a god—Apollo	0.0147
Having the body of a god—Buddha	21.33
Being under 5'2" (female)	16.083
Being under 5'2" (male)	36.083
Being over 6'5" (female)	33.127
Being over 6'5" (male)	8.878
Being over 6'5" and hating basketball (male)	29.24
Being pear-shaped	31.75
Being the Elephant Man	40.555

BOOGER

Being married to someone nicknamed "Booger"	18.921
Being nicknamed "Booger"	4.143
Finding a booger on the underside of a desk in a classroom	15.97
Having an impacted booger in your	

nose while you're in public and can't pick it | 7.33

BOSSES

Quitting a job when the boss has been really nice to you | 22.45

Working for a boss who blames you for his/her mistakes | 38.211

Working for a boss who has no life and doesn't expect you to have one | 40.441

Working for a boss who lies | 45.33

Working for a boss who thinks you're a slave | 50.2

Working for a boss who thinks you're a slave in his harem | 55.221

Working for a boss who will only promote his/her relatives, and you're not one of them | 57.44

Working for a boss who's stingy | 26.84

Working for an insecure boss who likes to keep his underlings fighting each other | 60.432

BREAKDOWNS

Being asked for a breakdown of an expense report that you padded | 28.98

The S-Factor Stress Gram Counter

Car breaks down at night in a strange state	16.77
Car breaks down when you can't afford to have it repaired	28.221
Car breaks down when you're in a rush to get somewhere	31.5
Having your car break down in a tunnel	65.44
Having your printer break down when you have a major project to deliver	25.77
Having your washing machine break down with your favorite clothes in it all wet and soapy	17.09
Having a nervous breakdown	62.987

BREAKFAST

Being in England and knowing that breakfast is the best meal you'll get all day	13.62
Breakfast at Tiffany's	18k
Drinking coffee while driving to work and spilling the scalding fluid into your lap at 60 MPH	55.55
Going to a breakfast meeting with a boss who doesn't eat breakfast	21.74

Having a roach stroll out of the cereal box	25.777
Having no milk for that first cup of coffee of the day	85.99
Squirting yourself in the eye when you dig into a grapefruit	37.91
The milk you pour on the last of your cereal is curdled	52.8
Your kids make you breakfast in bed, complete with runny egg whites, and you feel you have to eat it	19.447

BREAKING UP

Breaking up with a boyfriend/girlfriend—not your idea	32.541
Breaking up with a boyfriend/girlfriend—your idea	12.52
Breaking up with a boyfriend/girlfriend—your idea—and being stalked	48.3
Breaking up with your Siamese twin	88.88

BREAKS

Breaking a limb doing something illegal	65.3

The S-Factor Stress Gram Counter

Breaking a limb doing something stupid	38.23
Breaking a limb doing something sporty	17.322
Breaking some bones	53.22
Breaking some bone china	5.82
Breaking a shoelace	2.1
Breaking something that belongs to someone else	39.152
Breaking wind just at the moment when everyone else in the room is silent	27.44
Having your strand of antique pearls that your great-great-great-grandmother gave your mother's mother's mother break over the top of a sewer grate	64.32
When the toy you gave your own kid breaks within the first 30 seconds after he/she got it	18.42
When the toy you gave your sibling's kid breaks within the first 30 seconds after he/she got it	12.42

BURNS

Burning yourself with a match	8.321

Burning yourself with an acetylene torch	38.43
Burning yourself with a small nuclear device	83.211
Doing aerobics for an hour and not feeling the burn	10.2
Getting a rug burn while you're having an affair	19.331
Getting a sunburn	9.2
Having your house burn down	83.118
Turning on the light switch just as the bulb burns out	4.886
Being compared to George Burns	75.22

BURPING

A burp with chunks in it	4.12
Burping in front of a group of strangers	3.93
Burping in front of a group of friends	7.47
Burping in front of a loved one	8.31
Burping in front of your boss	9.272
Burping on a first date	10.37

BUSINESS

A competitor lures away your largest customer	27.9

The S-Factor Stress Gram Counter

Being asked for a bribe—money	37.225
Being asked for a bribe—sexual	49.225
Being the target of a hostile takeover by another company	43.222
Being the target of a hostile takeover by organized crime	53.222
Having a loony customer file a complaint with the local BBB	65.8
Having your friends and relatives do business with your competitors	12.45
Having your friends and relatives expect discounts	7.95
Having your friends and relatives expect free stuff	10.45
Starting your own business	49.228
Losing your own business	69.32
Selling your own business for a major profit	59.51
The annual audit	21.445
Your largest customer goes bankrupt owing you for a whole year	67.9

BUSYBODIES

Getting caught using drugs by

someone who wants you to go to a ten-step program	28.17
Getting caught using drugs by someone who wants to blackmail you	38.17
Getting caught using drugs by someone who wants you to share	8.17
People who ask how you "really" feel	17.4
People who offer unsolicited advice on how to raise your children	19.82
Your mail is censored by your warden	13.8
Your mail is stolen by your neighbor	27.4
Your mail is read by your mother	33.72

CAMP

Being given a swirlie (lowered head-first into a toilet which is then flushed)	52.1
Being sent to camp	20.544
Being sent to weight-loss camp	28.12
Being sent to a camp for promising artists	29.12
Being sent to boot camp	43.6
Being victimized by the old warm-water trick	47.2
Having a snorer in your tent	24.98

The S-Factor Stress Gram Counter

Having to call all your counselors "Uncle"	12.82
Having to eat unidentifiable meat	9.25
The archery instructor is nearsighted	29.21

CAR

Bumper stickers that tourist attractions put on your car	27.92
Car breaks down when you're in a rush	31.5
Not being able to start a car on a freezing cold morning	15.299

CAR ACCIDENT

Filling out police reports on a car accident	17.92
Hitting a cat that belongs to your child	77.286
Hitting your neighbor's cat	53.22
Hitting a deer	60.388
Hitting a duck	42.97
Hitting a large endangered animal	66.32
Hitting a person	86.2
Hitting a snake	4.88
The accident isn't your fault, but no	

one has any sympathy for you because you weren't wearing your safety belt	31.845
The accident isn't your fault, but the other driver is a lawyer	44.29
The accident isn't your fault, but you're in a state where they automatically jail drivers, right or wrong	79.331
The airbag deploys and your glasses break	22.812
The airbag doesn't deploy and your head breaks	54.77
You swerve to miss a dog and hit a tree	51.92

CAR BUYING

A car salesman who pretends to be your friend	6.65
Sticker shock on buying a new car	48.2
All the extra stuff they pile on while you are still suffering from sticker shock	15.76
Being trapped in a little office with the expert who's trying to "close" you	39.97

The S-Factor Stress Gram Counter

CAR DENTS

The first dent in your new car, caused by you	43.99
The first dent in your new car, caused by a friend or relative	38.64
The first dent in your new car, caused by a stranger you don't see who leaves a note with no name or address	35.82
The first dent in your new car, caused by a stranger you catch and can sue	18.432

CAR KEYS

Being charged $40 for a new car key	11.56
Locking your keys in the car	15.81
Locking your keys in the car and the dog's inside with the windows up on a hot day	19.332

CAR REPAIR

Being approached by a salesman trying to sell you a new car when you bring your car in for a repair	10.42
Being told that the warranty only covers the parts, and that you still have to pay over $500 for labor	18.342
Getting a dealer recall notice the day	

before you're due to start a cross-country trip	22.51
Getting your car fixed when the mechanic makes three times as much per hour as you do	28.9
Getting your car fixed when you don't understand anything about how cars work	30.66

CAR SELLING

Selling Aston Martins	4.007
Selling BMWs	321i
Selling Mazdas	626
Selling Yugos	42.86

CAR THEFT

Your car is stolen	44.83
Your car is stolen and used in a crime spree	55.2
Your car is stolen and used in a crime spree, and the thieves are so dumb they catch them by tracing the calls they made on your car phone	38.09

CARD REJECTED

	19.8

The S-Factor Stress Gram Counter

CASTRATION

Being psychologically castrated by your mother	64.81
Being psychologically castrated by your father	56.74
Being psychologically castrated by your spouse	38.5
Being psychologically castrated by your therapist	78.94
Being psychologically castrated by your boss	32.6
Being psychologically castrated by your cleaning person	41.77
Being castrated when the car you're parked in is hit	56.14
Being castrated by a territorial panda	51.886
Being castrated by a golf accident	43.8

CATS

Your cat decides to attack your new baby	49.3
Your cat upchucks a furball	8.91
Your cat upchucks a furball in front of your dinner guests	18.443

Your cat won't let your boyfriend into the house	21.8
Having to watch a plotless English musical for the third time to keep out-of-town guests happy	19.87
Your cat needs a $4,000 operation and you can't say no	32.77
Your cat gets your underwear from the laundry and brings it out to show guests	22.75
Having to put your cat in the traveling box before a trip	33.90
Not putting your cat in the traveling box for a short trip to the vet and the cat gets carsick	30.65
Having to watch your cat struggle with one of those lampshades they put on cats to keep them from scratching their ears	9.76

CHANGING

Changing a diaper	5.73
Changing a diaper—your own	65.22
Changing a flat tire at 12 noon	17.32
Changing a flat tire at 12 midnight	29.3

Changing schools	38
Changing your address	39.2
Changing your brand of cigarette	7.2
Changing your brand of gasoline	1.32
Changing your gender	77.43
Changing your job	29.221
Changing your name	23.72
Changing your pacemaker	83.66
Changing your political affiliation	2.01
Changing your profession	58.2
Changing your religion	33.97
Changing your toner cartridge	5.22

CHEATING

Learning that your loved one is cheating on you, from an acquaintance	51.28
Learning that your loved one is cheating on you, from a friend	51.28
Learning that your loved one is cheating on you, with a friend	88.534
Discovering your loved one is cheating on you by catching him/her in the act	63.56
Discovering your loved one is	

cheating on you with someone of his/her same sex	69.69
Discovering that your loved one is cheating on you, when you were already cheating and looking for a way out	11.28

CHILDHOOD

A parent lectures you about drugs while drinking a very dry vodka martini with a twist	18.5
Being a child of divorce and having to move from house to house	32.9
Being a latchkey child	11.724
Having a child while you are still a child	42.9
Having to eat your vegetables before you can have dessert	6.443
Having to wear the dorky clothes that your grandparents give you	39.443

CHORES

Washing the dishes	8.65
Washing the dishes and breaking one of the good ones	18.53
Washing the car	12.21

Cleaning the gutters	4.54
Cleaning the toilet bowl	5.32
Clearing a blocked toilet drain by plunging it	7.54
Clearing a blocked toilet drain by snaking it	8.5
Clearing a blocked toilet drain by siphoning it	9.44
Clearing a raccoon out of the basement	12.4
Clearing a wasp's nest from the eaves	13.112
Climbing a tree to trim a branch	12.7
Defrosting the freezer	2.77
Doing the laundry	16.4
Dusting	1.65
Getting a skunk out from under the porch	13.88
Making the bed	1.67
Shopping for food	10.44
Vacuuming the house	5.634
Vacuuming the pets	8.26
Calling your deaf aunt	3.99

CHRISTMAS

Christmas if you're broke	15.9

Christmas if you're Jewish	3.2
Discovering Santa doesn't exist when you're a child	14.54
Discovering Santa doesn't exist when you're an adult	32.87
Not believing in Christmas but wanting gifts anyway	10.5
Not getting what you wanted for Christmas	30.62
Swapping gifts with someone and discovering your gift is cheaper and cheesier	31.932
CIRCUMCISION—FEMALE	
Circumcision by father	62.54
Circumcision by mother	62.54
Circumcision by witch doctor	60.23
Self-inflicted circumcision by sequined panty hose	61.8
CIRCUMCISION—MALE	
Circumcision by a doctor	5.65
Circumcision by a gardener	49.48
Circumcision by a golf pro	49.42
Circumcision by a lover's teeth	45.43

Circumcision by a rabid feminist	64.33
Circumcision by a mohel	5.01
Circumcision by a shortsighted mohel without his glasses	65.00
Circumcision by Lorena Bobbitt	95.8
Circumcision by shark	90.33
Self-inflicted circumcision by zipper	87.4

CIRCUS PERFORMER

Being a high-wire flyer	29.5
Being a mime	1.66
Being shot from a cannon	39.29
Being the guy who sweeps up after the elephant parade	22.12

CLOTHES

Accidentally shrinking your favorite sweater	8.32
Deciding what clothes to wear for a big date	18.21
Deciding what clothes to wear for a big date when you are color-blind	26.33
Discovering you left a Magic Marker in your pants/blouse/skirt pocket in the washer	24.28

Discovering you left a paycheck in your pants/blouse/skirt pocket in the washer	27.02
Getting a run in your stocking	8.9
Getting a run in your stocking on your way to an interview	13.55
Leaving your own clothes in the dressing room while you go find a mirror	13.773
Making sure your clothes don't clash	7.92
Picking the right accessories	5.88
Pulling on a little loose thread and having a whole seam come apart	12.72
Realizing that all the pants in your closet have elastic waistbands	34.852
Realizing you have to iron your blouse/shirt two minutes before you have to be out the door and on your way to work	35.88
Realizing your entire wardrobe is out of fashion	18.98
Realizing your wardrobe has come back into fashion	3.764
Trying on a bathing suit in a communal dressing room	17.291

The S-Factor Stress Gram Counter

Underwear that's too small	18.8
COHABITATION	
Being anal compulsive and living with someone who has no sense of time	92.86
Living with someone who leaves dirty clothes all over the house	58.02
Living with someone who hangs lingerie all over the bathroom	57.23
Living with a bathroom hog	11.86
Living with a morning person and you're a night person (or vice versa)	39.23
Living with someone on a special diet	21.743
Living with someone who always keeps the toilet seat in the wrong position	15.6
Living with someone who forgets to give you messages	18.23
Living with someone who has a different favorite TV show that's on the same time as yours	39.75
Living with someone who hates your pet	37.13

Living with someone whose ex-flames keep calling	30.41
Living with someone who's on the night shift	28.4

COLLEGE

Having to pay for your child to go through college	38.39
Having to take courses in college that you already took in high school	13.91
Mandatory political correctness training	16.72
Not being able to register because your father "forgot" to pay the tuition	32.886
Staying awake studying an entire week before exams	42.7
Working full-time while going through college	41.64
Working full-time while going through college, and not getting a better job after you graduate	52.556

COMMUTING

Commuting to work by bus	6.7
Commuting to work by subway	10.4

The S-Factor Stress Gram Counter

Commuting to work by subway and having to stand	9.387
Commuting to work by subway next to a guy humming along with a Walkman	13.923
Commuting to work by subway and it breaks down between stops	14.64
Commuting to work by subway in Tokyo with cult members	34.7
Commuting to work by railroad	4.66
Commuting to work in a car alone	6.332
Commuting to work in a car with a broken air-conditioning system	12.54
Commuting to work in a car with a blow-up doll to take advantage of the HOV lane	1.002
Commuting to work in a car with a broken gas gauge	15.7
Commuting to work in a car with current books on tape	4.22
Commuting to work in a carpool	10.64
Commuting to work in a carpool with a reckless driver	15.7

Commuting to work in a carpool with someone who has body odor	18.99
Commuting to work in a carpool with someone who's always late	22.03

COMPUTERS

Buying your first computer	14.8
A power surge crashes your computer	53.88
Being put on hold for 4 hours by the tech support people	42.55
Being put on hold for 4 hours by the tech support people located in another time zone and then having to talk to someone who treats you like you're an idiot	61.5
Computer goes down while you're working on a major project	64.532
Computer goes down while you're working on a major project, and you neglected to back up along the way	84.123
Finding an error in a document you have already sent	41.812
Finding an error in a mailing you printed 50,000 copies of	82.7
Installing new software	8.9

Installing new software, and it doesn't take	17.33
Losing a computer file	21.372
Not knowing what RAM stands for	5.99
Shutting off the computer before saving the file you've worked on for an hour	30.5
Wading the Internet with a slow modem	21.724
Waiting for data to go from the computer to the printer	9.7

CONDOS AND CO-OPS

Being interviewed by a choosy acceptance committee	28.633
Being unable to sell your unit because the board has raised the maintenance fee too high	31.75
Living in a building where the board plays favorites	13.8
Living in a condo where nosy neighbors interview your guests	17.99
Living in a condo with a petty dictator as board president	21.485

Losing equity in your apartment because the board mismanages repairs	28.6
CONSTIPATION	
Being constipated for a day	6.73
Being constipated for a week	15.86
Being constipated for a month	66.8
COOKING	
Cooking for yourself	1.2
Cooking in a tiny kitchen	5.8
Cooking for your family	6.38
Cooking dinner for adult guests	9.4
Cooking dinner for adult guests and your boss	13.554
Cooking dinner for the boss only	15.885
Cooking for a girl/boyfriend	18.43
Cooking dinner for kids	7.2
Cooking for an anorexic teenager	20.6
Cooking with dull knives	7.221
Starting dinner and realizing you don't have a key ingredient	13.93
Cooking in a bug-infested kitchen	19.543
Being in the middle of meal	

preparation and discovering one of your ingredients is spoiled, rotten and/or bug-infested	13.57
Being in the middle of meal preparation and discovering one of your ingredients is spoiled, rotten and/or bug-infested right after you've mixed it in with the other ingredients	19.5
Cooking a soufflé while construction is going on next door	12.88
Cooking dinner and realizing that not everything will be ready at the same time	14.955

COWBOY

Being a cowboy	12.66
Being a cowboy with really bad allergies	18.721
Being a cowboy with really bad hemorrhoids	49.321
Dating a cowboy	14.8

CREDIT

Being offered credit by a bank that tried to repossess your house two years ago	13.21

Having your credit card turned down	21.7
You finally appear in a movie and they misspell your name in the credits	23.95
Your boss takes credit for your brilliant idea	21.28

CRIME

Being arrested	60.82
Being on the jury at the trial of a murderer	12.85
Being on trial for murder	64.7
Being stopped by the police	55.93
Being stopped by the police and being body-cavity searched	67.6
Coming home from vacation to find your house burgled	44.82
Getting a speeding ticket	48.953
Having the guy who mugged you and whom you testified against let off on a technicality	63.24
Having your driver's license revoked	54.8

CULTS

Joining a cult	14.62
Having a parent join a cult	51.66

The S-Factor Stress Gram Counter

Having a spouse join a cult	58.7
Having a spouse join a cult you already belong to	8.7
Dealing with people who want to recruit you for their group	27.363
Ecstasy-induced group hugs	17.8
Going through past-life regression and finding out that you used to be a peasant	38.111
Having your aura cleansed	21.96
Hearing someone you respect start talking about extraterrestrials	8.33

DEATH

Death of first parent	99.3
Death of first parent, if you never said, "I love you"	103.756
Death of first parent, if you're responsible for death	90.43
Death of first parent, if you were secretly praying for the death	6.66
Death of a parent who liked a sibling better	78.84
Death of second parent	71.229

Death of second parent and you finally get your inheritance	60.994
Taking care of second parent after death of first parent	68.269
Death of a spouse	95.8
Death of a grandparent who leaves you a fortune	32.8
Death of a grandparent who's poor	58.22
Having a younger sibling die	75.874
Having a younger sibling die—of old age	77.385
Death of a close family member	83.7
Death of a best friend	80.32
Death of a close friend	37
Death of a family pet	60.93
Death of a family pet, when you had to tell the vet to put "Fluffy" down	69.54
Involuntary manslaughter	55.033
Murder one	12.23
The death of Jerry Garcia (if you're a Deadhead)	88.9
The death of Elvis Presley (if you believe he's dead and care)	7.14

Hitting the button that launches the nuclear strike that ends civilization as we know it	89.94
Death of 300 people in a country you've never heard of	6.2
Death of an ex-spouse	1.032
Death of a pen pal	13.3
Death of a salesman	.03
Death of a Salesman—having to watch the play	8.43
Death of a Salesman—having to write a paper on it	37.97

DEBT

Disagreement about how much you owe on your credit card	60.42
Disagreement about how much you owe the IRS	65.923
Disagreement about how much you owe a loan shark	68.15
Disagreement about how much you owe your success to your parents	82.11
Maxing out all of your credit cards	19.8%
Owing money at 18% when all the	

banks will give you on your money is 4.5%	9.141
Owing more on your home than it's worth	23.66

DEMOLITIONS EXPERT

Being a demolitions expert	62.99
Being a demolitions expert in Ireland	65.9
Being a demolition expert with the DTs	76.543
Insuring a demolitions expert	76.922
Your angry ex is a demolitions expert	85.33

DENTIST

Going to the dentist	29.23
Being asked a question while your mouth is full of cotton	4.243
Getting a filling	6.8
Getting braces when a child	33
Getting braces when a teenager	66.32
Getting braces when an adult	47.21
Having an important meeting after your mouth has been numbed by the dentist	18.42
Having to listen to elevator music in a dentist's waiting room	28.292

Hearing the words "This may hurt a bit"	46.8
Root canal surgery	51.723
Waiting in a dentist's office with nothing to keep your mind off of the mindless Muzak but a forty-year-old booklet called "Be True to Your Teeth . . . And They Won't Be False to You!"	28.87
Being a lion dentist	63.94

DIARRHEA

Getting diarrhea	9.45
Getting diarrhea while running a marathon	34.6
Getting diarrhea while running a marathon and having it broadcast on national TV	69.9

DIET

Thinking about going on a diet	4.83
Realizing you'll never fit back into your high school uniforms	9.22
Discovering the restaurant doesn't have artificial sweeteners	11.8
Dieting	30.6

No-pizza diet	18.632
No-caffeine diet	24.22
No-salt diet	29.211
No-sugar diet	32.56

DISAGREEMENT

Disagreement with your child about body piercing	50.172
Disagreement with your child about going to a punk rock concert	44.16
Disagreement with your child about homework	36.906
Disagreement with your child about his/her drug use	61.823
Disagreement with your child about your past drug use	70.42
Disagreement with your child about toilet training	39.93
Disagreement with your spouse about finances	48.41
Disagreement with your spouse about having children	42.74
Disagreement with your spouse about hogging the blankets	87.172

The S-Factor Stress Gram Counter

Disagreement with your spouse about religion	38.92
Disagreement with your spouse about his/her parents	45.887
Disagreement with your spouse about where to live	41.95
DISASTERS	
Experiencing a flood	58.21
Experiencing a flood and there's no potable drinking water	88.92
Experiencing a forest fire	48.122
Experiencing a forest fire that you started by accident	88.38
Experiencing a tidal wave	50.96
Experiencing a tidal wave and your surfboard's in the shop	55.84
Experiencing an earthquake	67.93
Experiencing an earthquake and you're a collector of expensive china	87.93
Getting snowed in in Peoria	70.32
DISCOVERIES	
Discovering the FBI has a file on you	10.5
Discovering you're infertile	61.97

Discovering you're adopted	79.23
Discovering your loved one is a spy	28.23
Discovering your loved one is a spy for another government	49.312
Discovering your loved one is a transvestite	38.123
Discovering your loved one is a transvestite and he/she looks better in your clothes than you do	74.5
Discovering your loved one had a sex-change operation	83.91
Discovering your parents have rented out your room	36.82
Discovering that someone left only a few flakes of cereal in the box	19.6

DIVING

Taking your first dive	37.44
Taking your first dive in a boxing match	68.38

DIVORCE

Getting divorced	73
Paying child support	19.32
Paying alimony	29.21

The S-Factor Stress Gram Counter

Ex didn't send the alimony	67.32
Ex didn't send the alimony on time	65.4
Ex sent alimony in pennies	69.001
Ex uses your hard-earned money to travel around the world	75.43
Ex refuses to sign some papers needed for your taxes	42.78
Ex calls the IRS and convinces them to do an audit on you	57.8
Ex insists on dividing up your mutual friends	25.75
Ex insists on dividing up your mutual friends—with an ax	50.50
Ex publishes a best-selling kiss-and-tell book about your relationship	35.35
Ex remarries	40.32
Ex remarries someone younger than you	45.89
Ex remarries someone more successful than you	52.74
Ex remarries someone more successful than you who is eager to put your kid(s) through college	10.24
Ex remarries and they use your old bed	35.6

Ex shows up drunk at your wedding	151
Ex shows up drunk at your office	1.51
Ex shows up drunk at your parents'	0.151
Ex tells the kids lies about you	32.642
Ex tells the kids the truth about you	21.321
First date since the divorce was official	34.09
First sexual encounter with someone post divorce	30.54
Having your ex win the lottery	45.85
Having your ex win the lottery right after you've signed the settlement papers	59.22
Having your ex win the lottery when that means you can stop paying alimony	16.853
Having your ex win the lottery, and getting to sue for back alimony	21.574
Your child gets divorced	34.03
Your child gets divorced and you liked the spouse	44.211
Your child gets divorced and you hated the spouse	12.96
Your parents take your ex's side against you	38.7

Your parents ask your ex to move in with them	74.678

DOCTOR

Training to be a doctor	39.21
Training to be a doctor, and the cadaver sighs	44.8
Being a doctor specializing in proctology	13.521
Finding out the doctor isn't even in the building after you've been waiting for three hours	33.9
Getting a series of rabies shots for a raccoon bite	54.12
Going to the doctor for a physical and being forced to wear a skimpy gown that ties inconveniently in the back and doesn't properly cover your butt	31.88
Hearing the words "This may hurt a bit"	28.32
Not really being a doctor, but playing one on TV	0.23
Operating on a patient and having him/her die	84.32

Sewing up a patient and realizing a surgical instrument is missing	89.42
Sitting with a bare butt on a cold metal table	11.3
Taking a three-year-old to the doctor	23.89
The gynecologist holds an impromptu meeting with colleagues in the room while you're in the stirrups	38.96
The lab screws up a test and you have to have it redone	7.82
Waiting 4 hours to get to see your preferred provider doctor	22.55
Waiting a week to get the results of a test	13.743
Your doctor insists on an expensive procedure, but your HMO won't pay for it	42.76
Your first physical exam that includes a rectal examination	19.4
Hearing the words "You'll have to speak to the doctor to get your results."	44.2

DOGS

Cleaning up after your dog poops	7.33
Cleaning up after your dog poops inside	10.2

The S-Factor Stress Gram Counter

Coming home from work and discovering that your dog dumped the garbage all over the place	18.22
Having to take your dog out on the wettest day of the year	11.765
Having to wake up early just to take your dog out	14.35
Living in a city and owning a dog	9.77
Taking your dog for a walk, having it poop and forgetting the pooper scooper	13.712
The cost of pet food	8.221
The cost of having to cook for a pet that won't eat pet food	16.84
The cost to your back of carrying pet food	10.175
Your dog catches a porcupine	28.467
Your dog catches a skunk	43.2
Walking the dog	3.87
Washing the dog	9.71
Washing the dog who found a skunk	19.4
You have to have your dog put to sleep	79.13
Your dog runs away	59.23

Your dog runs loose and is kidnapped by drug research people	89.54
Your dog vomits in front of your dinner guests	43.18
Your dog vomits in front of your dinner guests, and then eats it	51.77
Your dog won't let your boyfriend into the house	37.6
The dingo dogs eat your baby and no one believes you	68.98

DREAMS

Dreaming about having to take a big exam that you haven't prepared for	41.57
Dreaming about hot dogs chasing donuts through a deserted copper mine shaft	35.46
Dreaming about making love to someone else while your significant other is asleep by your side	49.335
Dreaming you're naked in public	71.8
Dreaming you're drowning	82.55
Dreaming you're flying	49.42
Dreaming you're naked and running down your high school corridor	17.87

Dreaming you're naked and running down your high school corridor, then realizing you're not dreaming	47.09

DRIVER'S LICENSE

Expiration of your driver's license	10.2
Expiration of your driver's license, when a new picture is required	16.92
Flunking your driver's test	21.93
Flunking your driver's test on the third try	32.523
Having your driver's license revoked	54.8
Hitting another car while taking your driver's test	41.73
The first license on which you need glasses	20.20

DRIVING

Falling asleep at the wheel	0.12
Abruptly waking up as your car straddles the shoulder	84.12
Driving at night	10.2
Being behind someone who drives 55 MPH in the fast lane	29.35

Driving in Europe on the wrong side of the road	16.43
Driving in the middle of a steady downpour	30.64
Driving in the middle of a snowstorm	48.32
Driving in midtown Manhattan on a Wednesday afternoon	76.11
Having your parent teach you to drive	74.28
Sitting in a traffic jam	12.53
Sitting in traffic jam with a carload of kids who insist on singing "A Hundred Bottles of Beer on the Wall" and it's the middle of summer and the air-conditioner doesn't work and you have a splitting headache because your sinuses are acting up and you forgot to take your allergy medicine	52.43
Going on a long drive	10.34
Going on a long drive with kids	19.22
Going on a long drive with kids in a used Volkswagen Bug	38.231
Going on a long drive with kids in a used Volkswagen Bug through the desert	54.46
Going on a long drive with kids in a	

used Volkswagen Bug through the desert along with a grandparent who's incontinent	77.98
Missing an exit off the interstate	27.132

DRUGS

Having to take a drug test for a job when you can't remember how long ago you had your last joint	58.3
Writing the Great American Novel while on acid and waking up to find it unreadable	22.11
Getting high on pot and then being told you were smoking oregano	13.96
Having to watch people inject drugs in hip movies	22.98
Trying to talk to people on drugs	13.76
Having to listen to the preaching of born-again Christians/nonsmokers/former alcoholics/ex–drug addicts/UFO advocates	42.75
Having to tolerate naive morons who think that a slogan like "Just Say No" can take the place of social programs in combatting drug dependency	42.75

The flood of prostate/baldness/antidepressant drug ads in the paper	6.94
Not having an aspirin when you need one	32.08
Headache remedy ads that cause headaches	25.81
Discovering that your child's houseplants are marijuana	29.62
Discovering that your child drinks alcohol/uses drugs	51.95
Discovering that your child has found your drug stash	67.43
EATING	
Being forced to eat a Spam-based dessert by your cousins	48.27
Being forced by peer pressure to eat anchovies on your pizza	29.4
Being forced to eat live monkey brains to show you understand the local customs	51.7
Being forced to eat your words	60.32

The S-Factor Stress Gram Counter

EDUCATION

First day of school	60.32
Not getting into the fraternity/sorority of your choice	38.11
Not getting into your first choice of college	31.96
Paying for your child's college education at a community college	21.75
Paying for your child's college education at a state college	28.42
Paying for your child's college education at a private college	47.13
Sending your child off to college freshman year	42.85
Sending your child off to college after freshman year	3.66
Your brilliant child is being flunked by incompetent teachers	38.23
Your brilliant child is being given A's by incompetent teachers who are letting him/her coast and do no work	38.23

ELECTRICIAN

Being an electrician	12.8
Being an electrician in Sing Sing	29.33

ELEVATORS

Being trapped in an elevator	19.4
Being trapped in an elevator, and you're claustrophobic	84.85
Being trapped in an elevator with a claustrophobic person	67.43
Being trapped in an elevator without anything to read	72.443
Being trapped in an elevator without anything to read accompanied by a manic accordion player	92.375

EMBARRASSMENTS

Arriving at a party dressed inappropriately	34.51
Arriving at a party empty-handed	21.7
Arriving at a party too early	11.52
Being laughed at when you're angry	15.7
Having a comic single you out from the rest of the audience as the butt of his jokes	26.32
Moaning the wrong name in the middle of sex	32.98
Moaning "Mommy" in the middle of sex	35.83

Your parents showing your date your nude baby pictures	39.316
ENGAGEMENT	
Getting engaged	40.55
Shopping for the engagement ring	45.2
Deciding how and when to present the engagement ring	23.69
Telling your future spouse's parents you're engaged	37.33
Telling your future spouse's parents you're engaged, knowing they hate you	55.71
Telling your parents you're engaged	30.511
ENTERTAINING	
Dealing with a drunken guest	29.51
Discovering a guest is allergic to the main course	31.7
Having someone show up at your home without calling first	9.9
Hosting a cocktail party	14.964
Hosting a dinner party	21.6
Not having enough silverware for your dinner guests	23.6

Running out of food	39.53
The first fifteen minutes of a dance party you're hosting and no one's shown up	78.4
Waiting for guests to arrive	41.43
Going to an important dinner and being served something you don't like	10.3
ENTERTAINMENT	
Going to a movie	4.21
Having someone tell you the end of the movie before you've seen it	13.53
Renting a video	2.66
Renting a video and discovering you've already seen it	13.7
Watching a Merchant-Ivory movie	0.86
Watching a James Bond movie	0.007
ERROR TYPE 1 OCCURRED	14.99
EXERCISING	
Working out	5.32
Aerobics—thinking about them	7.434
Aerobics—doing them	11.65
Aerobics—taking a class that's far beyond your capabilities	39.5

Doing the stationary bike and being forced to watch something you don't like on TV	21.865
Getting on the stationary bike at the health club and discovering the person who used it before you neglected to wipe sweat off the seat and handlebars	25.75
Waiting to use the weights at the health club	8.24

EXPIRATION

Expiration of your health club membership	2.5
Expiration of your life	0.00

FAIL

	41.44

FALLING

Being a fall guy	29.54
Being a summer guy	1.645
Falling in a mud puddle	23.8
Falling in a mud puddle on your way home from work	20.53
Falling in a mud puddle on your way to work	48.212
Falling in love	41.87

Falling out of a window	67.86
Falling out with a friend	30.53
Ice cream scoop falls off of cone	8.33
FAMILY	
Having to visit Aunt Gertrude	18.86
Having to kiss Aunt Gertrude	22.49
Having to look at Aunt Gertrude in the coffin at her wake	30.12
Being asked to bring a younger sibling along on a date	35.62
Shouting so your grandparents can hear you	9.77
Having to thank relatives for insultingly stupid gifts	13.27
Being put on the phone with a niece who can't talk yet	6.28
Having to hold back on seconds at dinner when guests are over	7.12
Having to wear hand-me-downs	10.42
Your brother-in-law asks for a loan	14.87
FARMER	
Being a farmer	9.4
Being a farmer, and having some	

The S-Factor Stress Gram Counter

recently graduated county agent tell you you're doing everything wrong	17.73
Being a farmer, and seeing the property next to yours auctioned	32.96
Being a farmer, and seeing the property next to yours auctioned, and getting the equipment real cheap	20.64
Being a farmer on a small family farm	32.96
Being a farmer paid by the government not to grow stuff	7.86
Trying to dress stylishly while being a farmer	67.97

FARTING

Farting in front of your date	55.83
Farting in front of your boss	28.43
Farting in front of a group of friends	25.54
Farting in front of a group of strangers	19.6
Farting in front of a loved one	9.6

FAT

Getting too fat for your clothes	38.421
Getting too fat for your chair	43.89
Getting too fat for your doorway	58.3

FEMININE HYGIENE

Confusing the feminine hygiene spray and the breath spray	16.22
Discovering that extra-super-jumbo tampons are no longer big enough	39.53
Discovering that last month's tampon is still in place	45.876
Having the string break off of your tampon	35.22
Having your son run into the living room while your in-laws are visiting using your tampon case as a toy gun	60.33
Spilling your Evian in your purse and having your spare tampons inflate to the size of cantaloupes	31.34
Those times when you don't feel, well, fresh	11.34

FINANCES

Being overcharged	30.53
Comparing your income to Bill Gates's	76.64
Discovering how little you got in your first paycheck	22.75
Doing your taxes	39.66

The S-Factor Stress Gram Counter

Having to pay for major invasive surgery	77.86
Having your car repossessed	78.82
Opening your mailbox and finding a bundle of bills	20.29
Paying bills	21.7
Receiving a call from a collection agency	60.44
Receiving an overdue bill	18.71

FIRED

Being fired	47
Being "let go"	47
Being "downsized"	47
Becoming "redundant"	47
Being "outsourced"	47
Being "given liberty"	47
Being "given the opportunity to make an outward, lateral career move"	47
Being fired by a jerk who refuses to use the word "fired"	49.75
Being fired by someone you hired	58.85
Being fired by a computer	45.32
Being escorted out the door by an	

armed security guard when you are fired	50.5
Being fired because the company needs to find the funds to pay for the chairman's trips to Paris on the Concorde	48.32
Being fired, but being given a two-year severance package	40.44
Being fired for a suggestion you made	54.92
Being fired so the boss can give your company stock to his mistresses before the big buyout	61.43
Being fired the day before the bonuses are handed out	70.7
Being fired when you've already lined up the next job and you'll get to collect double pay for three weeks	30.831
Being fired when you were going to quit anyway	22.87
Being on a jury for the fraud trial of the CEO of the company that just fired you	10.88
Getting a call from a reporter about the company that just fired you	11.66

Getting a new job where the spouse of the jerk who fired you works for you	9.59
Hearing the words "It's for the best" as you are being fired	50.62
Being fired when you are a CEO and your contract calls for a $10 million severance package	0.932

FIREMAN

Being a fireman	30.4
Being a fireman in a town where punks like to call in false alarms	35.85
Being a fireman who's a woman	38.53
Being a fireman who's afraid of heights	56.9
Being a fireman who's allergic to smoke	67.282

FIRSTS

Being with someone on their first day of driving	21.43
Bungee jumping for the first time	43.71
First day of driving	23.532
First day of football practice	8.76
First day of marathon training	6.65

First day of prison	68.32
First day of retirement	21.63
First day of school	29.54
"First day of the rest of your life"—hearing that phrase	2.77
First day of therapy	43.212
First day of unemployment	48.41
First day of work	26
First divorce	73
First experience of impotence	45.42
First hemorrhoid	62.573
First marriage	31.74
First time you have sex	30.52
First use of alcohol	10.45
First use of coffee	8.353
First use of decaffeinated coffee	1.84
First use of drugs—if they are good drugs	0
First use of tobacco	16.66
First time in an airplane	29.52
First time parachuting	51.63
First time snorkeling	13.9

Prozac—first day on	35.33
Prozac—first day it kicks in	1.33
Prozac—first day off	66.43
Sending your child out alone on an errand for the first time	31.67
Greeting your daughter's first date	48.611
Waiting for your daughter to get home from her first date	66.41

FLYING

A 1-hour taxi to the gate after you land	32.88
A 1-hour wait before takeoff once the plane is loaded	30.721
A 1-hour wait before takeoff once the plane is loaded, and the air-conditioning is turned off	41.9
Arriving at the airport five minutes before your flight leaves	55.754
Being in the last row to be served	18.53
Being airsick	59.221
Being bumped from a flight and getting cash	19.42
Being bumped from a flight and getting vouchers for more flights on the same incompetent airline	23.634

Being bumped from a flight because you forgot to bring identification and you'd forgotten that terrorists have made airports get so security conscious that you practically have to get strip-searched before they let you on plane	38.54
Being caught in the traffic loop in front of the terminal for 50 minutes as your flight time approaches	33.69
Being caught stealing one of those cute little blankets	31.72
Being hijacked to Cuba	40.51
Being hijacked to Rochester	45.756
Being on a hijacked plane and hearing that the U.S. government is negotiating with the terrorists	44.65
Being on a long flight when a mass attack of food poisoning occurs	60.74
Being in the airplane bathroom when the plane hits an air pocket	34.2
Being stacked up and waiting to land	21.978
Being stacked up and waiting to land, and running out of fuel	32.54

The S-Factor Stress Gram Counter

Being strip-searched because a buddy called in your description to security	54.73
Being told at the gate that your luggage is too big to be carried on board	37.1
Cheery in-air pilot announcements of mechanical problems	41.53
Flight delayed 20 minutes	14.73
Flight delayed 1 hour	21.43
Flight delayed 3 hours	39.432
Flight delayed so you'll miss your connecting flight	48.81
Flight canceled	49.64
Having a seat that won't stay up	11.9
Having seen the movie before	7.32
Having the middle seat	9.8
Having the seat next to the bathroom	10.53
Having three hours to kill at the airport because you had to leave that much time to be sure you got there	9.16
Having your luggage be the last to come off the conveyor	20.3
Not getting a seat on a plane despite the fact that you had a reservation	15.92

Flying with a small child	33.98
Sitting next to someone with a small child	28.43
Sitting near a preteen with Nintendo and the volume is all the way up	19.77
Sitting next to a salesman	11.83
Sitting next to a drunk salesman	81.83
Sitting next to someone who can sleep on planes when you can't	18.54
Sitting on the aisle side of a 300-pound lady with a weak bladder	31.8
Some jerk took your limo because it has Bud Lite	23.98
Surviving a crash	87.98
Surviving after a crash by eating your fellow passengers	99.23
The dork behind you kicks your seat all flight	34.8
The drive home takes longer than the flight did	45.53
The passenger next to you gets airsick	56.43
The passengers who got on before you have used up all the overhead storage space	17.64

The plane you're traveling in suddenly drops 10,000 feet in altitude	67.3
They lose your luggage	72.11
Unscheduled stops	38.86
They run out of booze	87.9
Your ears block up during landing	21.98

FOOD

Finding a hair in your food	32.76
Finding a fingernail clipping in your food	53.7
Finding a finger in your food	77.98

FORGETTING

Forgetting a dentist appointment	0.21
Forgetting to take your lunch to work	7.82
Forgetting what year Columbus sailed	14.92
Forgetting your phone number	12.12
Forgetting your address	77.12
Forgetting your mantra	23.1

GOLF

Totally missing the golf ball on a drive	38.645
Totally missing the golf ball on a drive while playing on your boss's team	44.32

Totally missing the golf ball on a drive while playing against your boss	8.72

GRAFFITI

Stupid graffiti	2.88
Mean graffiti	4.994
Mean graffiti that mentions you	10.62
Mean graffiti that includes your phone number	20.632

GRANDPARENTING

Your grandchild abandons the family name	33.86
Your grandchildren want to know about parts of your past that are better left hidden	41.7
Having to eat with your grandparents who hate spices and eat dinner at 4:30 P.M.	34.8
Having to kiss your dead grandparent good-bye in an open-coffin viewing	76.29

GYM CLASS

Not being able to climb the rope	10.28
Being able to climb the rope, but not being able to get back down	21.8

The S-Factor Stress Gram Counter

Falling on the floor and getting a floor burn on your knee	13.8
Falling on the floor and hitting your funny bone	18.54
Not being able to do a push-up	15.743
Not being able to shoot a basket	12.6

HAIR

Dying your hair the wrong color	39.53
Getting a bad hair weave	29.6
Taking a shower and the water shuts off while you're in the middle of washing your hair	63.5
Wearing a toupee	21.64
Wearing a toupee in a tornado	73.7
Having a really bad hair day (male)	11.23
Having a really bad hair day (female)	41.75

HAZING

Being a freshman at a military academy (male)	33.56
Being a freshman at a military academy (female)	73.56
Being a homosexual freshman at a military academy	73.56

Being a masochistic homosexual freshman at a military academy	3.56
Being forced to eat a urinal cake by the frat boys	62.231
Taking a crap and discovering the frat boys have Jell-O-ed your toilet	32.665

HEALTH

Remembering to take your vitamins	7.54
Discovering your vitamins can cause cancer	21.7
Eating your minimum daily requirement of vegetables	4.343
Remembering to drink 8 glasses of water a day	13.755
Drinking 8 glasses of water a day while on a road trip	28.4

HEARING

Hearing the words "Your license and registration, please."	44.5
Hearing the words "Open up, it's the police."	52.76
Hearing the words "Are you asleep yet?"	19.55

The S-Factor Stress Gram Counter

Hearing the words "Don't take what I've got to say the wrong way, but..."	15.62
Hearing the words "Hang on, let me show you how to do this."	12.21
Hearing the words "Hi, I'm from *60 Minutes*."	41.75
Hearing the words "Your money or your life."	81.53
Hearing the words "If you have a Touch-Tone phone, press 1."	8.32
Hearing the words "It happens to every guy at one point or another."	45.21
Hearing the words "Let me share this with you."	7.54
Hearing the words "Let's just be friends..."	33.654
Hearing the words "Talk to my lawyer."	27.8
Hearing the words "When I was a kid..."	3.87
Hearing the words "You'll only feel a little sting."	21.3
Hearing the words "How do you really feel about that?"	22.19

Hearing the words "Because I said so."	55.32
Hearing the words "Is it safe?"	54.98
Hearing the words "This may hurt a bit."	28.32
Hearing the words "Margin call."	60.93
Hearing the words "Your call is very important to us . . ."	15.45

HEMORRHOIDS

Having hemorrhoids	30.7
Having to hear about hemorrhoids	11.84
Having to watch commercials about hemorrhoids	16.8

HOLIDAYS

You can't remember a thing that happened on New Year's Eve	39.42
You wake up next to someone you've never seen before on New Year's Day	41.66
The groundhog doesn't see his shadow	0.43
The groundhog sees his shadow	0.44
You receive a Valentine's Day card from an unknown admirer	10.3
You don't get one single Valentine's Day card	19.44

You forgot where you hid all the Easter eggs	17.8
April Fool's Day	21.7
April Fool's Day, if it's your birthday	42.6
Caught in traffic right after watching 4th of July fireworks	38.43
No one realizes that you have a Halloween costume on	18.65
You discover the Thanksgiving turkey won't be done for 3 more hours	26.866
Not getting a pony for Christmas or Hanukkah when you've been really good all year	31.56

HOME

Buying a new house	66.812
Calling a plumber	31.64
Calling an electrician	32.01
Cleaning your house	7.423
Decorating your house	10.22
Discovering a leaky faucet	13.53
Discovering a leaky roof	41.7
Getting a mortgage	41.53
Having a rodent loose in your house	28.192

Having construction done on your home	30.6
Having construction done on your home while you're living there	39.6
Living in a city	22.75
Living in a co-op	18.5
Living in a condo	14.996
Living in a country where your first language is not the predominant language	27.85
Living in a tenement	30.55
Living in the country	10.5
Living in the slums	68.32
Living in the suburbs	19.9
Living next door to a neighbor whose teenage son plays the drums	27.921
Living next to a disco	41.7
Living in sin	32.85
Being evicted	83.21
Being turned down by a co-op board for unspecified reasons	64.523
Realizing that the construction work is going to take twice as long as you thought	37.75

Realizing that the construction work is going to take twice as long and cost twice as much as you thought	47.2
Answering the door and finding a salesperson	14.53
Answering the door and finding a Jehovah's Witness	16.3
Painting a one-story house	25.63
Painting a two-story house	31.564
Painting a three-story house	46.13

HOUSEPLANTS

Forgetting to water your houseplants	13.6
Overwatering your houseplants	12.88
Experiencing the death of a houseplant	16.92
Discovering your houseplants have a disease	11.73

HOUSE-SITTING

House-sitting for a friend and all the plants die	9.53
House-sitting a friend's pet while he/she is on vacation and the pet dies	14.21

Deciding whether to tell your friend that his/her pet died while he/she is

on vacation or wait for him/her to get back	55.91
House-sitting for a friend and the place burns down	49.64
Facing your friend after he/she has returned from vacation and finds out about the death of the pet or the place burning down	76.9

ILLNESS

A major illness	53
Being sick	29.64
Being sick while on vacation	37.8
Being sick while uninsured and unemployed	43.9
Catching pneumonia	23.77
Chemotherapy	67.97
Contracting a deadly disease	84.98
Dealing with a sick child	21.8
Dealing with a sick baby	29.53
Dealing with a sick teenager	40.6
Dealing with a sick spouse	33.8
Dealing with a sick spouse who's also a hypochondriac	42.5

The S-Factor Stress Gram Counter

Ebola	99.8
Ebola when you had to diet anyway	90.42
Getting a cold	21.7
Having a head cold and being unable to hear	13.75
Having a head cold and being unable to hear your mother-in-law	8.98
Having major surgery	64.767
Having an accountant decide how many days you get to stay in the hospital to recover from major surgery	52.32
Having to take care of someone who has just had major surgery	59.32
Poison ivy	21.85
Sick parent	33.86
Sick parent who wants to move in with you	40.632
Terminal illness	89.86
INCOMPLETE	8.54
INJURY	
Spraining your ankle	13.8
Spraining two ankles	26.7
Breaking your nondominant arm	32.75

Breaking your dominant arm	47.43
Having 2 broken arms	82.97
Wearing a cast on your arm	31.87
Wearing a cast on your leg	42.4
Wearing a cast—full-body	71.32
Wearing a cast—full-body, and having fleas	82.86
Wearing a neck collar	41.7
Wearing braces on your legs	62.431
Wearing braces on your teeth	32.64
Wearing a Band-Aid	0.4
Having a bad back	48.654
Having a bad back, and getting full disability payments for it	27.38
Having a hangnail	1.97
Jamming a finger	5.86
Paper cut	.983
Paper cut—a really bad one	2.02
Pinching your privates in the zipper	35.56
Being in a wheelchair	38.6
Being in a wheelchair in San Francisco	49.33
Being in a wheelchair at a beach	63.76

Stubbing your toe	3.77
IN-LAWS	
Arguing with a mother-in-law	43.87
Being nice to your spouse's obnoxious siblings	15.7
In-laws expect you to help rearrange furniture while you're there	11.94
In-laws rearrange your furniture while you're out	18.1
Discovering one or more of your in-laws spent time in a mental institution	19.4
Discovering that one or more of your in-laws served time	24.12
Hearing that your mother-in-law drove off a cliff in your new car	50.50
INSURANCE	
Buying life insurance	33.76
Finding an affordable HMO	22.86
Discovering your spouse bought an insurance policy on your life—without consulting you	77.123
Filling out 37 forms to recover the money you spent	31.4

Filling out 37 forms to recover the money you spent, and still being denied	39.3
Finding out that the insurance company's accountants allow your doctor a lower hourly wage than the mechanics at the local BMW dealership	39.887
Having to discuss your mental or physical problem with some glorified HMO receptionist in order to get an authorization for treatment	31.46
Paying your own health insurance	42.18
Having your work pay for your health insurance	2.18
Talking to an insurance salesperson who calls him/herself an investment counselor	21.13
Thinking about life insurance	30.4
Waiting on hold for the HMO	29.37
Discovering your doctor gets a cash reward for not ordering an expensive test that could save your life	44.653
INVALID PASSWORD	60

JAIL

Going to jail	63

Going to jail when innocent	78.81
Going to jail and having to share a cell with an ax murderer	34.65
Going to jail and having to share a cell with an evangelist	66.6
Going to jail for the first time and you're really cute	71.5
Going to jail knowing you're guilty, but also knowing that the authorities haven't discovered half the crimes you've committed	28.21
Going to one of those cushy white-collar "Club Fed" jails the Watergate criminals went to	21.84

JOB

Asking for a raise	34.544
Being demoted	33.33
Being demoted while your rival gets a promotion	66.66
Getting a severe salary cut	39.33
Dealing with a boss	20.64
Dealing with a boss who's dumber than you	35.63

Dealing with a boss who's dumber than a stick	5.779
Discovering at an important business meeting you have something caught between your teeth or a booger on the tip of your nose	39.22
Having your boss over for dinner	34.853
Discovering your coworkers have been invited to your boss's for dinner and you have not	54.76
Experiencing downsizing survivor's guilt	55.95
Firing someone	45.6
Firing a U.S. postal worker	90.210
Going on a job interview	33.09
Having to go to the bathroom in the middle of a job interview	9.3
Having to go to time management classes when you have lots to do	23.54
Having to make an important business call from home the same day the kids are on vacation	28.5
Inadequate job recognition	31.98
Inadequate resources to do the job	36.8

The S-Factor Stress Gram Counter

Inadequate pay	38.08
Increased workload	15.4
Increased workload without increased salary	29.53
Losing a job	47
Working on a big business report on your computer that's due the next day and your lover comes in the room with a nice cup of cocoa but he/she trips over the corner of the rug and spills the steaming hot liquid on your leg and, as you jump up in shock, you inadvertently pull the plug to the computer out of the outlet with your foot and lose the entire document and, by the way, you had neglected to back the damn thing up	44.92
Major project due in one month	10.837
Major project due in two weeks	10.838
Major project due in one week	10.839
Major project due next morning	68.844
Shipping your package to its destination in time	4.87
Shipping your package to its destination using FedEx	1.54

Shipping your package to its destination using UPS	12.6
Shipping your package to its destination using that other carrier	54.482
Too damn much work	30.8
Unclear job description	21.75
Working a 60-hour week	26.7
Working 9 to 5	18.98
Working the graveyard shift	34.21
Being handed a 200-page document without page numbers	5.6
Being handed a 200-page document without page numbers, and dropping it	15.65
Coping with a cute secretary/administrative assistant you have the hots for and want to take out on a date and he/she knows it	22.69
Coping with a secretary/administrative assistant suffering from low self-esteem	3.87
Coping with a secretary/administrative assistant who wants a promotion	30.482
Coping with a secretary/administrative assistant who's the boss's kid	43

Coping with an inept secretary/administrative assistant	14.5
KIDNAP	
Being kidnapped and your spouse refuses to pay the ransom	74.34
Being kidnapped by aliens	72.92
Trying to convince the government you've been kidnapped by aliens	83.8
LAUNDRY	
Doing the laundry	16.4
Running out of quarters for the Laundromat dryer	19.5
Having someone else handle your undies at the Laundromat	27.3
Your mother does the laundry for you when you visit home and she irons permanent creases into your favorite pair of jeans	25.99
LAWYER	
Being a lawyer	23.86
Being a lawyer with a conscience	94.77
Being an ambulance chaser	7.22
Being married to a lawyer	27.95

Dealing with a condescending lawyer who assumes you are too dumb to understand your own case	46.92
Dealing with a lawyer who encourages you to sue someone you like	63.752
Dealing with a lawyer who insists on using lots of Latin terms	51.92
Living with a lawyer who views every conversation as an argument	31.93

LENDING

Lending a book out and not getting it back	8.41
Lending a favorite article of clothing to a friend	10.45
Lending money to someone who "forgets" to pay you back	16.432

LOCKER ROOM

Taking a shower in front of others	12.96
Taking a shower in front of others and being tormented by sadistic jocks snapping towels at you	20.923
Taking a shower in front of others and dropping the soap	43.854
Your teammates discover you're the	

The S-Factor Stress Gram Counter 105

one who put heat balm in their jock straps before the game	23.72
LOCKING	
Locking your keys in the car	28.343
Locking your keys in the car, with the alarm on	41.47
Locking your keys in the house	25.81
Locking your keys in the house, with the alarm on	47.86
LOSING	
Losing one sock of your favorite pair	4.432
Losing the election for president of the class	21.93
Losing the election for President of the United States	63.92
Losing your child in a crowd—baby	84.92
Losing your child in a crowd—teenager	0.12
Losing your hair (male)	19.64
Losing your hair (female)	88.43
Losing your job	47
Losing your favorite pen	11.48
Losing your diary at work or school	59.345
Losing your religion	62.921

Losing your virginity	36.96
Losing your wallet	49.833
Losing $20 in a three-card monte scam	39.43
Losing all your teeth	71.95
Losing your nose to leprosy	81.9
Losing at Trivial Pursuit	11.92
Losing a parent	100
Losing a parent in a mall	8.34
Losing a paper clip	1.09

LOST

Being lost in a crowd	29.75
Being lost in the wilderness	32.83
Being lost in Bloomingdale's	62.865
Being lost in space	89.234

LOTTERY

Choosing numbers for your lottery ticket	2.21
Not winning the lottery	3.86
Winning the lottery	65.44
Winning the lottery and having your name and address announced so every	

charitable beggar and investment shill in the nation can pester you	10.432
Winning the lottery and not knowing where you put the ticket	91.55
Having your numbers win the lottery the one week you decided not to buy any tickets	44.75
Having your fellow employees pool together, buy a lottery ticket and win— and you weren't included	86.22

LOVE

Falling in love	18.34
Falling out of love	8.12
Falling in love with a fellow employee	16.42
Falling in love with your boss	19.33
Falling in love with someone who's married	22.54
Cheating on your lover	41.5
Having your lover cheat on you	41.503
Cheating on your lover by sleeping with his/her best friend	54.34
Getting a disease because your lover cheated on you	55.332
Having your mother be right about	

the lover who cheated on you and gave you a disease	61.453
Cheating on your spouse	42.5
Having your spouse cheat on you	42.503
Having a loved one walk in on you while you're with someone else	58.31
Having someone you love tell you he/she sees you more like a sister or brother	27.33
Unrequited love	30.4
Discovering love isn't a two-way street	38.32
LOW BATTERY	14.92
LYING	
Telling a little white lie	9.332
Telling a whopper of a lie	10.6
Telling a whopper of a lie, and getting caught	18.6
Being lied to by a parent	65.92
Being lied to by a spouse	50.37
Being lied to by a loved one	45.8
Being lied to by a boss	42.88
Being lied to by your child	41.734
Being lied to by a coworker	23.93

Being lied to by a realtor	1.329
Being lied to by a lawyer	0.03
Being lied to by a politician	0.02
Being lied to by a salesman	0.01

MANAGEMENT

Being threatened with a strike	69.4
Discovering that your favorite employee is stealing from you	52.865
Having to file EPA impact statements	38.21
Having to go through a whole long procedure before you fire someone who's incompetent	49.31
Having to make "reasonable accommodations" for unreasonable employees	54.1
Having to pay workers' comp to a guy who hurt his back bowling	41.54
Having your payroll stolen	83.12
Your biggest supplier goes out of business	57.32
Your biggest supplier changes specifications	62.95
Your biggest supplier raises prices	68.61

Your biggest supplier demands up-front payment	76.3
Your top salesman quits to start his/her own company	44.8

MARRIAGE

Getting married	50
A spouse who hangs lingerie all over the bathroom	16.94
A spouse who hangs sweaty gym socks all over the bathroom	16.94
A spouse who leaves dirty clothes all over the house	19.33
A spouse who won't let your friends come over	61.32
A spouse who gains forty pounds after the wedding	68.2
A spouse who no longer wants to have sex	73.42
A spouse who "forgets" he/she is married when in a bar	77.31
A spouse who repeats everything twice	21.21
A spouse who repeats everything twice	21.21
A spouse who doesn't respond when you're talking	30.21

A spouse who just doesn't listen!	81.9
Being the sole breadwinner	42.86
Coming home from a long day at the office and it's your spouse's turn to make dinner but your spouse "forgot" and you were counting on having something to eat because you didn't have time for lunch due to an important staff meeting you thought you could get out of but you couldn't and now you're so hungry you have one of those headaches and your spouse says, "Sorry," but that doesn't make you feel any less hungry so you get mad and yell that being sorry isn't enough and your spouse gets upset and you have a big argument and you end up sleeping on the couch, hungry	21.63
Trying to get something done when your spouse is procrastinating	48.42
Discovering your spouse is just like your parents	84.73
Having to be nice to your in-laws	29.34
Having to be nice to your spouse's boss	21.8
Having to hear your spouse's jokes over and over	71.64

Having a good friend marry someone you can't stand	39.31
Having your child marry outside of your religion	51.12
Having your child marry outside of your race	62.86
Having your child marry outside of your species	77.21
Mixed marriage	55.71
Non-mixed marriage	55.71
Each additional marriage for a Mormon	12.81
Your mother remarries and moves to another country	2.91
Getting home from work just in time to see that special TV program you've waited all day to watch and walking in the door to discover that your spouse's parents were in the neighborhood and decided to drop by and see their little "beauty" or "prince" and the "beast" he/she married and you have to make nice and you're cursing yourself because you never learned how to program the damn VCR	16.33

The S-Factor Stress Gram Counter

MEETINGS

A 2-hour meeting held totally in the dark so someone can show slides	8.12
A 2-hour meeting where you have a chair that makes fart noises when you move	14.66
A 2-hour meeting with no agenda	34.66
A 2-hour meeting where everyone has a secret agenda	44.66
Having to defend your department budget before the executive board	44.76

MENTAL

Realizing you're more screwed up than you thought	72.46
Being anal compulsive	48.75
Being anal compulsive and suffering from Alzheimer's	78.2
Being the only one in your office who's not on Prozac/Zoloft/Librium/Dilantin, etc.	13.86
Calling the suicide help line and being put on hold	49.12
Encountering a raving lunatic	51.96

Encountering a raving lunatic, and it's your shrink	72.57
Having multiple personalities, and you're not the one your spouse likes	31.31
Having multiple personalities, and you're not the one who likes sex	36.36
Having multiple personalities, and one of you is wanted by the police	45.45

MOVIES

The theater's popcorn is stale	5.12
Your feet keep getting stuck to the theater floor	4.555
A colorized version of your favorite movie	6.78
Your change falls out of your pocket just as the lights go out	8.433
The people next to you talk through the whole movie	10.67
A mouse runs across your feet halfway through the movie	13.98
Watching a movie in which an actor directs him/herself	13.99
Sitting next to Pee-wee Herman	17.62

MOVING

Moving yourself	59.231
Being professionally moved	21.86
The moving crew breaks all your china	62.68
Moving to the suburbs	20.53
Moving to a rural area	37.35
Moving to a major metropolitan area	55.233
Moving to a different country	72.68
The dogs in your new neighborhood terrorize your cats	48.3
The first call you get is from the producers of *Unsolved Mysteries*, who want to film at your house	41.03
The guy who sold you the house keeps coming home to his old house when drunk	38.42
The neighborhood is so tough they have a welcome tank instead of a welcome wagon	34.89
You discover your new house is built over an ancient Indian burial ground	82.74
You discover your new house is infested with rats	85.54

The new place is so small you have to give up your queen-sized bed	41.32
Your old landlord won't give you back your security deposit	21.94
You have to choose new doctors	21.4
You have to discover new cleaners	24.75
You have to learn a new zip code	9.78
You have to learn the layout of a new supermarket	56.974
You have to leave behind the doorway on which you marked your children's height every birthday	34.756
You have to reset all the buttons on your car radio	19.453
You have to reset all the buttons on your car radio and the only station that comes in is a 24-hour Elvis station	82.72
Being moved by the Witness Protection Program	81.46

NAMES

Being named Woody, Peter, Dick or Willie	12.43
Forgetting your date's name	42.9
Being named Newt	63.7

NEIGHBORS

Living next to a gun collector	20.43
Living next to a mental institution	22.211
Living next to a crack house	23.34
Having an upstairs neighbor with a hyperactive child	31.65
Having an upstairs neighbor with a hyperactive child who's learning to play the drums	47.86

NEWSPAPER

Reading the paper	10.57
Finding black ink all over your shirt after reading the paper	8.94
Having someone steal your newspaper from your front door	6.343
Needing glasses to read the newspaper	4.31
Ripping an article out of a newspaper and having it tear through the middle	14.467

NOISE

Fingernails on a chalkboard	31.35
Having a car alarm go off outside your window	18.8

The sound of one of your bones breaking	48.776
The steady drip-drip-drip of a leaky faucet	11.86

NURSE

Being a nurse	38.54
Being a nurse for an HMO	51.98
A nurse who can't find a vein	47.654
Having the catheter removed by an angry nurse	83.82

O.J.

AUTHORS' NOTE: By including the following section, we are in full compliance with the O.J. Act of 1995, which requires mention of O.J. Simpson in all works of social commentary.

Having to read about O.J. years after the damn trial	14.44
Being one of the few who think that O.J is innocent	14.98
Knowing that O.J. got away with it	14.98

The S-Factor Stress Gram Counter

Being married to a man who worships O.J.	24.53
Having your daughter date O.J.	51.02
Not being able to refer to orange juice as O.J.	1.55

PARENTING

Giving birth to your first child	51.7
Giving birth to your thirteenth child	0.13
Giving birth to twins	52.64
Giving birth to twins unexpectedly	78.232
Bringing up twins	22.2
Bringing up an average child	10.32
Bringing up a gifted child	31.76
Being a single parent	27.1
Figuring out what to make your child for dinner	8.212
Figuring out what to make your child for dinner, when you don't know how to cook	21.37
Discovering your child is anorexic	62.46
Discovering your child is anorexic, and it had nothing to do with your cooking	60.35
Finding a 666 birthmark on your baby	66.666

Getting children ready for school	23.54
Guilt over having been too lax with your child	29.4
Guilt over having hit your child	34.45
Having a child join a cult	52.57
Having a child who's a sleepwalker	11.45
Having a colicky baby	82.23
Being a father and talking to your teenage daughter about the facts of life and she asks you a question about menstruation and you start to stutter and break into a cold sweat because she wants to get your opinion on whether to use a tampon versus a sanitary napkin and she starts listing the pros and cons as she sees them and you're feeling more and more uncomfortable but you can't say that to her because you were the one who told her she could come to you and ask you anything she wished on the topic of sex	71.9
Having to explain the birds and the bees to your children	15.87
Helping the kid with math homework	3.14

The S-Factor Stress Gram Counter

Helping the kid with math homework, and not having a clue	98.34
Hosting a sleepover for your 9-year-old son and six of his friends	43.85
Leaving your child with a baby-sitter	7.12
Leaving your child with a baby-sitter for the first time	71.2
Listening to your children sing the themes to TV commercials	18.73
Missing your child's performance in the school play	29.53
Picking up your child from school when it's pouring outside	11.68
Realizing that—no matter what you do—you embarrass your child when you're around his/her friends	27.811
Realizing that you are in the middle of a meaningless battle with your child	34.9
Realizing you say "Because I said so" a lot	55.32
Realizing your child's right and you're wrong while in the middle of a heated argument	71.72
Talking to your child about drugs and alcohol	21.345

Teaching your child to drive	82.46
Being the parent of a child who insists on hitchhiking	42.5
Trying to fix your child's toy and breaking it by mistake	35.5
Trying to nurse a child with a sucking problem	41.12
Watching your child get a shot	57.312
Your child walking in on you while you're having sex	42.243
Your child walking in on you while you're having sex with someone other than your spouse	83.53

PARKING

Forgetting where you parked your car in a mega-mall parking lot	49.31
Parallel parking while no one is looking	4.523
Parallel parking while a crowd is looking	24.57
Parallel parking while Hell's Angels are watching to see if you hit their bikes	51.2
Pulling forward to parallel park and some jerk scoots into the space	12.476

PAST DUE	47.76
PAYING	
Paying for your sins	21.4
Paying your dues	48.221
Paying for your child's education	79.93
PERFORMANCE	
Forgetting your lines in the school play	32.34
Forgetting your lines at the altar	68.31
Forgetting your lines in a Broadway show	78.2
Losing your voice the day of the big performance	82.75
Not being able to have an erection	93.53
Not being able to have an orgasm	23.64
PET FISH	
You try and flush a dead fish and it keeps coming back	18.248
Your pet fish eat each other	21.786
Your roommate puts his hand in the tank	12.7
Your roommate puts piranhas in the tank because you like to put your hand in the tank	54.53

Your guests pour martinis into your carefully balanced saltwater tank	29.293
A power failure causes your tank to cool down 10 degrees	32.57
The raccoons discover your koi pond	35.82

PETS

Walking your dog early in the morning and it's cold and it's your day off and the dog takes 20 minutes to poop, then the dog tugs at the leash just enough to throw you off balance and the only way you can keep from falling on your butt is by stepping right in the middle of the dog's crap	29.21
Having a pet of the same gender as you "fixed"	43.68

PHOTOGRAPHS

Having your picture taken	6.92
Having your picture taken, and trying to act candid	14.5
Having your picture taken, and trying to act candid, and the damn photographer takes 10 minutes to focus the camera	29.32

Having your picture taken wearing a bathing suit	31.3
Having your picture taken when you're in bed with someone who's not your spouse	73.89
Having your picture taken and fearing that your soul has been captured	87.67

POLICE PERSON

Being a police person	23.78
Being a police person in South Central L.A.	37.778
Being a police person under pressure to back your corrupt buddies	42.67
Being a police person and hating donuts	54.3

POLITICS

Knowing the candidates will break all their promises	1.21
Not understanding what a referendum means	2.34
Knowing you should vote but hating both candidates	9.45

PORT-O-SAN

Having to use an overripe Port-O-San	5.831
Realizing that the Port-O-San has no roof and the construction crew three floors up is watching you	30.51
Having a Port-O-San picked up by a crane while you're using it	72.8
Having a Port-O-San tip over and spill on you	89.823

PREGNANCY

Becoming pregnant (female)	65
Becoming pregnant (male)	94.65
Getting someone pregnant, if you are aware of it	45
Getting someone pregnant, if you are not aware of it	0

PRESSURE

Pressure to be creative on the spot	47.31
Pressure to be a good parent	57.12
Pressure to be a good role model	64.9
Pressure to breast-feed	37.85
Pressure to breast-feed, if you're the father	86.5

Pressure to bungee jump	49.56
Pressure to date	28.63
Pressure to do drugs	40.23
Pressure to say no to drugs	65.74
Pressure to do well on standardized tests	51.4
Pressure to get into a good college	37.1
Pressure to get your baby into a good preschool	73.767
Pressure to give to the blood drive	10.23
Pressure to give to the United Way	2.78
Pressure to go along with the gang	37.123
Pressure to go to church	21.6
Pressure to have a baby	45.865
Pressure to have sex	36
Pressure to have your picture taken	7.23
Pressure to have your picture taken in a bathing suit	31.3
Pressure to sky dive	52.64
Pressure to start using the Internet	11.86
Pressure to vote	8.212
Pressure to write thank-you notes	3.785

PROFESSIONAL WRESTLER

Being a professional wrestler	12.56
Being a professional wrestler who's typecast as a baddie	23.623
Being a professional wrestler and having a ridiculous stage name	31.35
Being a professional wrestler and taking a dive	42.921

QUITTING

Quitting sex	6.9
Quitting school	20.53
Quitting a job	40.24
Quitting chocolate	61.33
Quitting drinking	62.68
Quitting heroin	65.26
Quitting a relationship	51.231
Quitting smoking	82.15
Quitting breathing	99.9
Quitting coffee	99.9

RECYCLING

Being caught throwing out your recyclable garbage along with your regular garbage	14.57

The S-Factor Stress Gram Counter

Being served warmed-over coffee	18.76
Being seen rummaging around a Dumpster for wood for your urban fireplace because you don't want to spend money on the firewood sold at the deli next door	28.464
Having to haul 3 huge trash bags of empty bottles to the store for a $1.70 refund	37.86
Being woken up in the middle of the night by someone digging loudly through your garbage for cans and bottles	33.6
Digging through someone's garbage for cans and bottles	41.47
Having to buy expensive disposable plastic plates because the store was out of paper plates	21.67
Dealing with all those damn, staticky Styrofoam packing peanuts	54.23
Deciding whether to throw the newspaper away before you get home so you don't have to tie it up for recycling	6.76
Dropping food on the floor and	

debating whether or not to pick it up, dust it off and eat it	38.215
Having to break down and tie up boxes for recycling	9.43
Hiding glossy-covered magazines in between the corrugated cardboard and newspaper	17.34
Running out of twine so you can't tie up your old newspapers	21.6
Waking up the next morning to discover it poured the night before and the sanitation department neglected to pick up all those now incredibly soggy newspapers	23.654
Marrying someone who was previously married	22.23
Marrying someone who knows his/her previous lives	25.23

RELATIONSHIPS

Asking someone on a date	24.351
First date	34
Second date	30.53
Third date	42.75
Blind date	46.86

The S-Factor Stress Gram Counter

Going on a date with someone you really want to impress and taking that person to a super-fancy French restaurant and you try to show off by ordering something in French and the waiter doesn't have a clue what you're talking about but you insist you know what you're saying and he shrugs his shoulders and brings you what you asked for and when he returns he plops down a plate with a filthy sneaker garnished with beets and brussels sprouts in front of your date, she gets really, really embarrassed and wants to leave and it's at that precise moment you discover you left your wallet at home	32.754
Starting a new relationship	36.57

RELIGION

Being a Southern Baptist and not knowing how to swim	24.68
Being a Trappist monk and getting caught talking in your sleep	56.9
Being bald and trying to wear a yarmulke	12.56

Being caught sleeping during the sermon	18.334
Being caught sleeping during the sermon because you've been snoring loudly	22.6
Being caught stealing from the collection plate	49.31
Born-again anything	41.75
Dealing with Hare Krishnas in the airport	6.66
Discovering your priest was once arrested for pedophilia	72.976
Forgetting the name of your godchild during the rite of baptism	41.68
Forgetting the Stations of the Cross	12.576
Forgetting to bring money for the collection plate	4.67
Forgetting your lines during Passover seder	10.4
Going to confession after a particularly sinful week	19.34
How your parents always set out Elijah's glass, even though he hasn't shown up for years, and you have to	

go hungry if you're 5 minutes late for dinner	9.52
The abortion issue	58.45

REMARRIAGE

Remarriage	42.32
Being compared to the ex	21.234
Being compared to the ex in bed	63.33
Disciplining the stepchild for the first time	43.123
Disciplining the stepchild for the first time, and the child's natural parent isn't around to offer support	45.5
Your father remarries a woman who wants your late mother's jewelry	51.55
Your father marries a young, buxom airhead and leaves her the estate	63.87
Your father remarries and moves out of your extra bedroom	18.43
Your father remarries someone who hates kids	55.45
Your father remarries someone whose kids are super-achievers	61.33
Your mother remarries in Scotland and wants you to pay your own way there	32.12

Your mother remarries a man chosen by her guru	67.79
Your mother remarries a retired Marine drill sergeant	75.34
Your mother remarries someone whose kids are real dorks	54.49
Your parent remarries to one of your teachers	70.43
Your parent remarries to your principal	82.1
Your parents decide to remarry for the fourth time	2.88
Your parents want you to pay for this wedding	55.34
Your parent remarries a cat person and you're a dog person	49.77

RESEARCH

Answering one of those phone polls that takes twice as long as they said it would	23.18
Dealing with research experts who refuse to draw conclusions	26.18
Having to do extensive research	34.602
Having to do extensive research, when your computer and modem are broken	44.602

The S-Factor Stress Gram Counter 135

Being caught after having faked your research	42.86
RESTAURANTS	
Going out to eat	3.24
Going out to eat with a bunch of friends and trying to decide where to go	5.76
Finding a table to sit at in a crowded restaurant	6.42
Waiting to order	7.33
Waiting to get your food	4.7
Waiting to get your food, and you're famished	21.52
Asking someone in a restaurant where the bathroom is and having that person point it out using sweeping hand gestures	7.13
Figuring out the tip at the end of the meal	8.25
Figuring out the tip at the end of the meal without using a pencil or calculator	82.5
Figuring out the tip at the end of the meal after drinking a bottle of wine	0.825

Figuring out what to tip the waiter in a foreign country	£12
Being ignored by your waiter	11.65
Being shown up for your lack of knowledge of wine by the sommelier	13.42
Having someone order for you in a restaurant	15.3
Being with someone who sends food back for no apparent reason other than to "impress" the rest of the table	33.58
Getting the check	9.32
Dividing the check equally (including tip) for a table of thirteen	36.45
Trying to get out of paying the check	15.67
Figuring out who ate what so you can divide up the check	24.231
Dining with people who insist on figuring out who ate what so you can divide up the check	30.31
Finding a hair in your food	32.76
Finding a pubic hair in your food	65.423
Getting takeout from your local Chinese restaurant and discovering when you get home that they gave	

you white rice instead of the brown rice you ordered	3.57
An expensive restaurant serves you lukewarm water for tea	15.73
Being seated at a table and discovering that the Heimlich maneuver instruction poster is on the wall directly in front of you	11.56
Administering the Heimlich maneuver to a choking patron in a restaurant	48.67
Choking on a piece of food in a crowded restaurant, being given the Heimlich maneuver and having the whole event taped and featured on the evening news	68.33

RETIRING

Retiring	45
Retiring voluntarily	40.83
Retiring involuntarily	65.492
Getting a gold watch and it breaks the next day	0.121
Not getting a gold watch	21.57
Living with someone who just retired	55.95
Realizing you can't afford to retire	59.76

Realizing you're bored stiff on the first day of your retirement	77.2
RETURN TO SENDER	7.932
REUNION	
Attending a 10th high school reunion	20.003
Attending a 20th high school reunion	8.934
Attending a 30th high school reunion	4.999
Attending a 40th high school reunion	2.881
Attending a 50th high school reunion	1.999
Attending a high school reunion, and you're the only one to show up	14.902
Attending a high school reunion, and your former best friend tries to sell you insurance	18.902
Attending a family reunion	5.934
Attending a Manson family reunion	46.98
Attending a family reunion, and bringing a lover	11.420
Attending a family reunion, and bringing a lover of the same sex	26.969
Watching the Brady Bunch reunion on TV	4.21

Rumors about the remaining Beatles getting back together	2.87

ROOMMATES

Your roommate has a gun hidden under his/her mattress	32.69
Your roommate has a KKK hood	49.43
Your roommate is a dealer	21.56
Your roommate is a hooker	0.8
Your roommate views you as a romantic possibility	13.78
Your roommate views you as a romantic possibility, and it grosses you out	33.78
Having your parents living with you	65.13
Living with a knuckle cracker	8.2
Living with a hard-of-hearing person who shouts	33.12
Living with a dog person and you're a cat person (or vice versa)	20.66
Living with a compulsive home shopper	41.94

RUNNING

Running for the train/bus/plane	21.53

Running the marathon	26.2
Running for office	41.675
Running for cover	52.97

RUNNING OUT

Running out of energy	7.33
Running out of clean underwear	12.45
Running out of milk for your coffee	23.64
Running out of coffee	99.9
Running out of gas	35.75
Running out of gas in the middle of the desert	73.56
Running out of gas with your date	2.21
Running out of time	42.876
Running out of money	62.34
Running out of Prozac	98.12

SALESPERSON

Being a salesperson	21. 89
Being a used-car salesperson	17.43
Being a salesperson who sells door-to-door	24.85
Being a pimp	29. 89

The S-Factor Stress Gram Counter

SCHOOL

First day of school	29.54
Getting your report card	21.656
Getting a bad report card	35
Getting caught in a food fight after you've just finished eating all your ammo	18.43
Getting expelled or suspended	39
A bully steals your lunch money	34.2
A bully steals your lunch money at gunpoint	72.86
Being brought up on charges of sexual harassment and you're only six years old	67.31
Being caught with a stash of Advil in your backpack	77.84
Failing a whole year of school	50
Failing a whole year of school so you can spend another year with a teacher you have a crush on	6.92
Having to wear a school uniform	11.53
Not having to wear a school uniform and having to figure out what to wear every day	10.54

Homework—being assigned a lot of it	21.63
Homework—actually doing it	41.24
Learning that your school is buying a bunch of metal detectors	49.54
Seeing the school bully walking toward you from the other end of the schoolyard	31.57
Taking an oral exam	19.4
Taking a written test	20.23
Taking the S.A.T.s	28.234
Taking a test you haven't studied for	34.75
The teacher really dislikes you	41.64
The teacher really likes you, and the other kids notice	49.45

SELF-EMPLOYMENT

Being nice to rude customers	15.53
Being unable to get disability insurance	14.434
Having the local cops ask for freebies	28.396
Having the local thugs ask you to pay protection money	31.85
Having to deal with long-distance service salespeople	36.5
Having to fill out business tax forms	49.213

The S-Factor Stress Gram Counter

Having to keep the store open on weekends	21.9
Having your friends and relatives give their business to the competition	31.68
Your largest customer asks for a bigger discount	22.65
Your largest customer asks for a blowjob	36.75
Your largest customer demands that you tie into their computer system	29.32

SELLING

Selling a happy customer on a new product	25.44
Selling a new product into an existing market	31.73
Selling a product designed for a foreign market	29.45
Selling an overpriced product	33.657
Selling bad products	35.2
Selling bad products to your relatives (a.k.a. "relationship marketing")	40.34
Selling bad products to yourself, because you're embarrassed to sell them to others	45.7

Selling buggy whips	65.23
Selling the number 3 product in the marketplace	48.234
Selling to a nonexclusive territory	28.34
Selling to a territory that's too big	33.67
Selling your customers on a price hike	41.67
Selling and your company won't let you have an entertainment budget	30.2
Selling and your manager decides to come along	47.21

SEPARATING

Separating from your spouse	59.242
Separating from your spouse when kid(s) are involved	68.53
Telling your family you're separating	50.4
Discovering your parents prefer the one you're separating from over you	76.32
Finding a place to live after separating	39.53
Finding a place to live after separating that's close to the kid(s)	41.57
Having to separate the potatoes from the beans on your picky child's dinner plate	21.98

Having to separate the runny egg white from your underdone eggs	21.98
SEX	
Having sex	20.56
Having sex—unprotected	40.845
Being a nymphomaniac	69.69
Dating a nymphomaniac	69.69
Faking an orgasm	22.4
Farting during sex	31.54
Farting during cunnilingus	52.76
Swallowing	26.976
Gagging during fellatio	41.23
Not having an orgasm	19.32
Premature ejaculation	39.023
The phone ringing during sex	10.53
Discovering you and your significant other are below the national average in number of times a "normal" couple is supposed to have sex in a given week	3.34
Realizing that you can no longer reach a sexual climax twice in a hour	10.069
Realizing that you can no longer reach a sexual climax twice in a week	25.069

Realizing that you can no longer reach a sexual climax twice in a month	39.069
Not having sex for 6 months	25.26
Being told you may have been given a sexually transmitted disease	73.6
Telling your grandparents you're gay	44.76
Telling your kids you're gay	51.45
Telling your parents you're gay	59.24
Telling your spouse you're gay	65.32
Discovering one of your siblings is gay	18.42
Discovering one of your siblings is gay and being the one who has to tell your parents	31.35

SHOPPING

Shopping	6.31
Shopping for clothes	8.422
Shopping in a crowd	11.6
Shopping the day after Thanksgiving	81.2
Shopping with a child	14.35
Shopping with children	19.22
Shopping with a child who's constantly grabbing stuff off the shelves and throwing it on the floor	22.645

The S-Factor Stress Gram Counter

Shopping with a child who's either too hungry or too tired	39.2
Shopping with a child who's screaming	41.43
Dealing with a pushy salesperson who's guilt-tripping you into spending more money than you intended or can afford	21.64
Grocery shopping	11.46
Choosing a grocery cart with one wheel that's stuck	11.24
Discovering the store is out of something on your list	7.23
Figuring out what's the best buy	5.39
Getting to the grocery store and realizing you've forgotten the list	15.35
Keeping your coupons straight and getting confused as to what size product is actually being offered at the discounted price	14.243
Waiting in the checkout line to pay for your groceries	8.31
Waiting in the checkout line and being caught reading the *National Enquirer* or *Soap Opera Monthly*	9.53

Waiting in the "10 items or less" checkout lane with 11 items	15.97
Waiting in the "10 items or less" checkout lane behind someone who has 11 items	29.01
Paying for your groceries	7.243
Not having enough money to pay for your groceries	20.24
Not having enough money to pay for your groceries and having to decide what to put back while a long line of irate customers gives you the evil eye	31.24

SHOT

Drinking a shot	4.55
Getting a shot	14.68
Getting shot	88.92

SHOWERS

Taking a shower and there's no water pressure	19.5
Taking a shower with no hot water	38.12
Taking a shower and the hot water runs out	43.8
Being scalded in the shower when someone flushes the toilet	19.23

Bridal shower	21.7
Golden shower	85.091
SIBLINGS	
Sibling rivalry	39.53
Realizing your parents love one of your siblings better	49.2
Having a younger sibling get a better job and earn more money than you	24.635
Having a younger sibling get married before you do	31.57
Having one of your friends date one of your siblings	11.89
Dealing with a sibling who's an escaped convict and who's come to hide out at your house	66.31
Having a sibling who's an ordained minister	6.66
Having a sibling who's an ordained priest and your parents think he's great but look down on you because you work in a paint store and spend your weekends at the disco	19.77
SLEEPING	
Sleeping during a church sermon	9.343

Sleeping during sex (female)	15.92
Sleeping during sex (male)	0.32
Sleeping in a freezing cold room	12.24
Sleeping in an overheated room	10.49
Sleeping in the room next to honeymooners	15.57
Sleeping next to someone who talks in his/her sleep	11.68
Sleeping on a jet plane	9.35
Sleeping while piloting a jet plane	84.21
Sleeping on a pullout couch	11.45
Sleeping on the wet spot	17.35
Sleeping on a subway grate	49.65
Sleeping on a train and missing your stop	56.24
Sleeping on the ground in scorpion country	71.46
Sleeping while a car alarm keeps going off outside your bedroom window	9.34
Sleeping while the faucet drips	16.24
Sleeping while driving and abruptly waking up as your car straddles the shoulder	84.12

Sleeping with no pillow	11.76
Sleeping with the lights on	7.32
Sleeping with the TV on	4.76
Sleeping with a cast on	24.77
Waking up to the alarm	18.325
Sleeping through the alarm	0.023
Discovering you've slept through the alarm	33.52
Experiencing a wet dream	21.856
Experiencing a wet dream, and your significant other is asleep by your side	34.57
Sleeping in the same bed as a dog you don't like	20.53
Sleeping in the same bed as a dog that doesn't like you	28.34
Sleeping in the same bed as a cousin who's a bed wetter	33.4
Sleeping in the same bed as a spouse you're arguing with	38.32
Sleeping in the same bed as a hacked-off horse head	82.68

SLEEPLESSNESS

Staying awake all night	21.93

Staying awake all night, and you have to make a major presentation the next day	32.87
Waking up early and not being able to get back to sleep on your day off	12.29
Waking up 10 minutes before the alarm goes off	8.23

SMOKING

Trying to quit smoking	82.15
Trying to learn smoking	16.98
Being a closet smoker	19.93
Being lectured by a nonsmoker	11.54
Being lectured to by a smoker who's recently quit	24.32
Trying to find a smoking area	26.94
Going to someone's home and asking whether or not you can smoke	21.76
Discovering the person you're interested in smokes cigarettes	29.43
Discovering the person you're interested in smokes cheap cigars	34.45
Lighting the wrong end of a cigarette	23.78
Lighting the wrong end of a cigarette	

when you're 15 and your friends are watching	23.78
Getting through that first meal without a cigarette for dessert	32.65
Going to a bar soon after you quit smoking and realizing you can't have a cigarette with your drink	45.675
Having great sex for the first time since you've quit smoking and then realizing that you can't have a cigarette	30.4
Needing a cigarette really badly and not having a light	29.21

SOCIAL

Making friends	10.76
Being interrupted	11.89
Being mimicked by a street mime with a crowd of people watching	15.67
Going to your spouse's company picnic	4.23
Going to your spouse's company picnic, and getting really drunk	39.31
Introducing your spouse to a group of people and forgetting someone's name	23.89
Introducing your spouse to a group of	

people and forgetting your spouse's name	73.89
Meeting people for the first time	8.2
Talking with someone whose sense of space is such that they get right up in your face	10.45
Talking with someone whose sense of space is such that they get right up in your face, and they have bad breath	21.6
Being chosen by the coven to bear the son of Satan	89.15
SORRY, TRY AGAIN LATER	20.81
SPANKING	
Spanking a child in the '50s	7.44
Spanking a child in the '90s	57.44
Spanking a client while dressed in leather	4.44
Spanking your monkey	3.44
SPECIAL EVENT	
Forgetting your anniversary/loved one's birthday	53.53
Remembering your anniversary/loved one's birthday that morning	62.312

Having to give a piano recital at age 6	13.57
Having to listen to a piano recital by a 6-year-old	19.433
Sitting next to a horn blower at a ball game	18.3
Bungee jumping	78.243

SPEECH

Speaking in public	83.12
Trying to speak over microphone feedback	88.99
Dropping your note cards as you walk up to the podium to deliver your speech	23.76
Having your grammar corrected when you're making an important point	42.67
No one laughs at any of the jokes in your speech	62.97
People start to leave in the middle of your speech	71.13
Someone asks you a question about the topic of your talk and you don't have a clue as to the answer	84.8

Someone in the audience interrupts your speech to inform you that you've

attributed a key quote to the wrong person	78.23
The audiovisual portion of your talk is missing	52.65
The electricity goes out in the middle of your speech and no one can hear you	36.12
The speaker before you covers all the points you were planning on covering and does a great job of it	79.223
The speaker before you gets a lot of laughs and a standing ovation	80.24
The speaker before you dies	27.34
You hear someone snoring during your speech	48.23
You realize just as you utter the first words of your speech that you have the hiccups	88.8
You start to laugh for no apparent reason in the middle of your speech and you can't stop	59.97
Instead of imagining everyone in their underwear while giving a speech, the only vision you have is you and you're naked	91.54

The S-Factor Stress Gram Counter

SPORTS

Thinking about starting to exercise	3.788
First day of exercise	15
Being beaten by a beginner at a game you're supposed to excel at	39.34
Making the team	18
Not making the team	28
Marathon training—1st day	17.23
Marathon training—2nd day	19.4
Marathon training—3rd day	42.865
Playing a team sport and standing out for making a game-winning play	31.75
Playing a team sport and standing out for making a supremely ridiculous play	37.2

STOCKBROKER

Working on Wall Street	30.42
Working on Wall Street, and being investigated by the SEC	31.04
Working on Wall Street during a stock market crash	83.68

STOCKS

The stock you decided not to buy soars sky-high	48.2

The stock tip you got proves to be a bust	12.5
The company you bought stock in is losing money, but the chairman's making $22 million a year	16.5
You make a profit, but not enough to cover the commissions	17.90

STRESSORS

Calculating every imaginable stressor	67.02

SURGERY

Being advised you need invasive surgery	58.423
Being prepped for invasive surgery, and they suggest you sign a blank organ donor release, "just in case"	76.432
Being prepped for invasive surgery, and they suggest Last Rites "just in case"	89.24
Being told the surgery they're planning has never been successfully done	92.84
Being told they took the wrong leg	94.46
Hearing the surgeon say "oops" while he's operating	96.3

SWIMMING	
Diving into a pool and your bathing suit comes down to your knees	28.235
Swimming and getting a cramp in your leg	11.32
Swimming in the ocean where people have been talking about the great white shark someone just spotted in the area	41.42
SYSTEM CONNECTION IS LOST	64.56
SYSTEM ERROR	73.921
TAXES	
Being taxed	37.3
Doing your taxes	39.66
Organizing a year of receipts	46.32
Preparing your own tax return	10.40X
Receiving a letter from the IRS	60.91
Discovering in the letter from the IRS that you are going to be audited	84.532
Discovering your accountant has been arrested for embezzling	69.23
Figuring out how much you can get away with claiming under the	

entertainment section of your tax return	14.57
Learning that your senator made millions last year but paid no taxes	44.87
Being told that the tax form directions have been written to be easily followed by a 5th-grader, and you are totally baffled	55.94

TEACHING

Teaching elementary school	30.53
Teaching high school	41.576
Teaching kindergarten	44.68
Teaching high school in an inner city school	72.6

TEEN YEARS

Having to be seen with a dorky younger sibling	18.42
Having your parents chaperone a party you're attending	30.53
Your father or mother insists on teaching you how to drive	65.12
Acne	73.7

The S-Factor Stress Gram Counter

TELEPHONE

A dinnertime call from a charity	5.56
A dinnertime call from one of the long-distance companies asking you to switch carriers	7.23
A dinnertime call from someone selling investments	8.422
A dinnertime call from someone selling investments, when you can't afford dinner	12.56
Being cut off by an answering machine mid-message	18.34
Busy signals	8.87
Dialing a fax number by accident and getting your ear blasted by the tone	10.354
Getting a phone call at 3 A.M.	39.6
Getting a phone call at 3 A.M. and it's a wrong number	30.54
Getting a recorded solicitation call	14.53
Getting caught calling those 900 numbers	41.69
Seeing the phone bill at the end of the month and realizing the majority of your calls were to 900 numbers	37.32

Having a 3-year-old hang up on you every time you call	15.34
Having a phone conversation with a 3-year-old	5.96
Having a phone conversation with a 93-year-old	5.96
Having some phone solicitation company constantly call your cell phone and you have to pay for it	35.7
Having your cell phone lose its charge halfway into an important phone call	29.342
Having your cell phone break down the first day of a 5-day business trip	44.23
Having your crazy former roommate use your remote codes to intercept your phone messages	33.755
Trying to keep the phone line free while living with a teenager	41.235
Trying to figure out which telephone company offers the most cost-effective long-distance service	8.35
Being beeped on the street and not having a quarter to check messages	15.37
Dealing with people who won't return calls	13.6

Having 23 voice mails to listen to	11.63
Trying to get off the line with a person when Call Waiting starts to beep	10.5
Trying to get off the line with your mother when Call Waiting starts to beep	34.8

THERAPY

Going to a therapist	21.85
Going to therapy for the first time	37.78
Coping with life while your therapist is on vacation for the entire month of August	42.567
Dealing with people who use the excuse of being an adult child to avoid responsibility for their own actions	40.8
Getting to your therapy appointment on time	11.58
Dealing with why you arrived late to therapy	39.3
Discovering your therapist has fallen asleep in the middle of your session	71.32
Discovering your couples therapist is divorced	15.31

Paying good money to a therapist who just repeats what you say	29.42
Seeing your therapist in the supermarket	37.75
Seeing your therapist in the supermarket fondling a cucumber	46.13
Sitting in the waiting room of your therapist's office and discovering that all the other people waiting to see their therapist are really messed up	32.68
Sitting in your therapist's waiting room and seeing him/her laughing quietly with another therapist as they surreptitiously sneak a number of glances in your direction	38.57
Sitting in your therapist's waiting room and seeing him/her laughing quietly with another therapist as they surreptitiously sneak a number of glances in your direction, and you're paranoid	96.923
Walking down the street and seeing your therapist with a woman and a couple of kids tagging along and realizing that this is his family, and his wife is not anything like what you	

fantasized in session with him and now that you know the truth it freaks you out and you go up to him to say, "Hi," and he only says, "Hello" in response, and it gets really awkward just standing there and he's not about to introduce his family to you so you get real embarrassed and mumble something silly and skulk off and when you're about 10 feet away you hear your shrink and his family start laughing but you don't have the courage to look back in their direction for fear they may be looking right at you | 66.23

Having erotic feelings for your therapist | 12.14

Telling your therapist you have erotic feelings for him/her | 32.54

TOILET PAPER

Toilet paper installed in the wrong direction | 10.55

Living with someone who cares what direction the toilet paper unrolls in | 13.15

Discovering you're trailing a piece of toilet paper on your shoe after a visit to the bathroom at a restaurant | 21.13

Discovering you're trailing a piece of toilet paper on your shoe after a visit to the bathroom at work	28.275
No toilet paper	84.8
Rough toilet paper	8.87
Scented toilet paper	3.432

TORTURE

Being tortured by a 2-year-old	72.01
Being tortured by a teenager	81.64
Being tortured by a junta	53.64

TRAVEL

Discovering you packed the wrong book	15.35
Forgetting to pack your toothbrush	18.23
Hailing a cab	6.353
Hailing a cab during rush hour	18.57
Hailing a cab in the middle of a torrential downpour	31.24
Missing a train/bus/plane	45.231
Missing your train/bus/subway stop	35.24
Traveling backward in a train	10.4
Packing for a trip the day before	11.24
Packing for a trip the night before	16.35

Packing for a trip 10 minutes before	28.896
Refolding a map	64.78
Not having exact change for the toll	6.55
Tossing coins and missing the exact change basket	21.24
Traveling alone	8.35
Traveling alone as a child	24.93
Traveling with 1 child	15.53
Traveling with 2 children	19.234
Traveling with 3+ children	27.12
Traveling with an obsessive-compulsive person	35.64

TRUCKERS

Being a trucker	8.3
Driving a cross-country haul	13.2
Learning to drive a tractor trailer	32.54
Driving a triple tractor trailer through midtown	43.23
Driving 16 hours straight	55.55
Driving 16 hours straight on amphetamines	80.80

TV

Cancellation of your favorite TV show	16.34
Deciding whether or not to get cable	5.35
Discovering all your TV shows are in reruns	11.57
Discovering that the sponsors of your favorite TV show include Preparation H, Efferdent, Depends and Hair Club for Men	60.60
Discovering your favorite TV show has been preempted for a silly Presidential debate	21.45
Figuring out what to watch on TV in the '90s	75.34
Figuring out what to watch on TV in the '50s	3.68
Getting the Sunday newspaper and discovering the TV section is missing	20.24
Getting the Sunday newspaper and discovering the TV section is missing, during the first week of the fall premiere-show season	43.72
Learning how to read the TV show listings	11.86
Missing your favorite TV show	12.7

The S-Factor Stress Gram Counter

Realizing you're addicted to cable	15.67
Seeing a commercial for a sweet, gooey, perfect-looking chocolate cake and realizing you have nothing sweet to eat in the house	31.46
Seeing the same TV commercial for the 50th time	67.94
TV commercials	9.43
TV commercials that are louder than the show you're watching	16.24
Waiting for a commercial so you can pee	29.82
Waiting for a commercial so you can raid the refrigerator	8.67
Having a desperate urge to pee while you're watching a commercial-free program on public TV	34.86
Watching a beer commercial the day after you decided it was time to go to AA	20.74
Watching TV while someone else controls the remote (male)	87.42
Watching TV while someone else controls the remote (female)	0.32

Fighting over who gets to control the remote	22.8
Losing the remote	28.34
Watching your favorite movie on TV and discovering they've cut out all the good lines	9.46
A network cuts off the last 2 minutes of a game you're watching	57.24
TWENTYSOMETHINGS	
Finding a job out of college	8.32
Finding a job out of college that pays more than minimum wage	43.86
Realizing if your mother hadn't thrown out your childhood toys, they'd be valuable now	20.01
Realizing if your mother hadn't thrown out your childhood toys, they'd be valuable now and you'd have enough money to move out	40.2
Your parents take over your old room	31.84
Your parents take your paycheck as rent	52.854

The S-Factor Stress Gram Counter

UNEMPLOYMENT

Waking up Monday morning and realizing you have no job to go to	10.53
Reading the Help Wanted ads	11.75
Paying for your own health insurance	87.33
Being asked to go out with your employed friends and realizing you can't afford it	28.53
Being unemployed, with a spouse who works	21.57
Being woken up at home by a prospective employer and it's after 9:00 A.M.	32.689
Writing a résumé	15.58
Writing an honest résumé	19.58
Discovering the job you're vying for comes down to you and someone else	26.86
Discovering the job you're vying for comes down to you and someone else from a very popular minority	41.7
Forcing yourself not to watch daytime TV while waiting for all those job offers to come in	23.545
Giving yourself a 3-hour lunch break	5.56

Giving yourself a 3-hour lunch break, but not being able to afford lunch	5.56
Going on an interview	20.74
Going on an interview, and being asked, "What are your strengths and weaknesses?"	25.92
Going on an interview, and sweating like a pig	30.64
Going to a party and having someone ask what you do for a living	22.57
Going to a party and having someone you're really interested in ask what you do for a living	31.23
Having an ignorant jerk tell you how to rewrite your résumé	18.8
Having to wait 6 weeks before getting your first unemployment check	22.92
Making follow-up phone calls	19.86
Meeting the jerk who fired you at the unemployment office	9.85
Having only one week left before your benefits end	43.2
Realizing, after you've been offered a job, that you're having second thoughts	

because it will mean you'll miss your daily soap operas	17.57

VACATION

Going on vacation	13
Going 1 year without a vacation	11.6
Going 2 years without a vacation	16.567
Going 10 years without a vacation	3.68
Going on vacation, and it rains 2 days out of 7	14.012
Going on vacation, and it rains 4 days out of 7	20.23
Going on vacation, and it rains all damn week	41.33
Calling into the office from vacation and the receptionist doesn't recognize your name	20.34
Camping vacation	17.74
Cruise vacation	9.34
Driving vacation	14.234
Free vacation	2.78
Having the office call you every day of your vacation	38.34

Not being able to afford to take vacation	21.712
Taking vacation when the boss really wanted you around	18.4
Using up your vacation time being sick	19.534
Using your vacation to paint the house	29.42
Using your vacation to visit the in-laws	83.3
Vacation with kids	31.044
Vacation with kids and pet	38.94
Vacation with 2 generations of family	18.35
Vacation with 3 generations of family	28.23
Returning from vacation	41.54
Involuntary vacation	65.35

VETERINARIAN

Being a veterinarian	30.34
Being Shamu's dentist	42.68
Having to tell someone that his/her pet should be put down	37.35
Having to tell someone that you put his/her pet down by mistake	61.5
Helping a prolapsed cow give birth	41.67
Helping a prolapsed cow give birth while the bull is watching	52.756

The S-Factor Stress Gram Counter

VIDEO

Renting a video	2.66
Renting a video, and discovering you've already seen it	13.7
You're psyched to see a certain video from the video store and someone has already taken it out	12.64
You go to the video store, find that the current hot video is available but then realize you don't have any money because you left your wallet at home	11.76
Forgetting your video club membership number	13.465
Going to the video store and discovering you've forgotten to "be kind and rewind"	9.45
Programming your VCR	31.854
Realizing you forgot to bring the video back and are going to be charged a day's extra rental	11.24
Discovering a rented video under the couch that you watched 3 weeks ago	31.46
Watching a program you taped and finding out that the tape ran out before the show ended	21.56

Watching a scary movie	24.19
Watching a video and finding that the good parts have been edited out	22.5
Being secretly videoed in the bathing suit changing room at Thong-a-Rama	41.35
Having to watch someone's wedding video	62.24
Having to watch yourself on *America's Funniest Home Videos*	21.56
Your VCR eats a tape	18.3
You are secretly videoed in your honeymoon suite but you don't discover it until your 10th anniversary when you decide to go back to the hotel where you spent that first night together as man and wife and celebrate by renting a porno movie and discover you two are the stars of the show	46.95

VISIT

One-day visit at your parents'	10.54
One-day visit at your your in-laws'	25.5
One-day visit from your parents	15.21
One-day visit from your in-laws	20.75
Entire week visit at your parents'	33.19

The S-Factor Stress Gram Counter

Entire week visit at your in-laws'	41.46
Entire week visit from your parents	29.35
Entire week visit from your in-laws'	38.98
VOMITING	
Vomiting when you are really drunk	31.46
Vomiting and having projectile diarrhea at the same time	39.33
Vomiting when you are on the whirly ride at the amusement park	43.77
Vomiting when you are on the whirly ride at the amusement park, and your boss is seated next to you	55.68
Vomiting while wearing a space helmet	71.57
WAITING	
Waiting in line	7.98
Waiting in line, and having an impatient person behind you	12.589
Waiting on line, and having someone cut in front of you and some obnoxious person behind you yells, "We're all waiting on line here!" and having the person who cut into the line not do anything, or worse yet have him/her argue back	39.54

Having to sit through a long service in a hot church or temple	15.76
Having to wait all day for an appliance delivery or repair person	29.51
Waiting 4 hours to see your preferred provider doctor, whom you haven't even met yet	31.57
Waiting a week to get the results of a medical test	21.823
Waiting a week to get the results of a school test	27.53
Waiting for mass transit	8.934
Waiting in an outdoor line	8.44
Waiting in an outdoor line, when it starts raining	11.87
Waiting in an outdoor line, when it starts raining and you're wearing a white silk blouse and no undergarments	23.97
Waiting in line at the Department of Motor Vehicles	54.7
Waiting in line for the men's room	3.21
Waiting in line for the ladies' room	43.98
Waiting on tables	10.92
Waiting for Godot	11.67

WEATHER

Changing a tire in the rain	20.34
Driving in fog	9.57
Driving in rain	12.46
Driving in snow	17.92
Walking through snow without boots on	31.6
Getting caught in a downpour without an umbrella	21.46
Having your flight canceled because of bad weather	38.68
Leaving the house in the morning without hearing the weather report for the day and realizing you are inappropriately dressed	8.23
Riding through a hurricane on a bike	38.89
Trying to convince your child it's not cool to chase twisters, no matter what they do in the movies	26.53
Being snowbound for 5 days when you are on salary	16.86
Being snowbound for 5 days when you are on commission	38.86

Suffering from seasonal affective disorder	45.87
WEDDINGS	
Picking the wedding date	28.23
Planning the wedding	65.74
Deciding whom to invite to the wedding	45.68
Weddings on a boat	43.68
Outdoor weddings	60.24
Getting married	50
Getting married at City Hall	48.56
Eloping	9.243
Giving away your little girl (female)	19.42
Giving away your little girl (male)	60.23
Shotgun weddings	78.76
Paying for the wedding	98.21
Finding out you've gained 10 pounds just before the wedding (male)	9.13
Finding out you've gained 10 pounds just before the wedding (female)	91.3
Having to go to the bathroom after you get the gown and veil on	44.44

Having to go to the bathroom just as the wedding march starts playing	49.03
Arriving late to your wedding	56.57
Choosing a wedding gift	11.46
Deciding how much to spend on a wedding gift	21.57
Surviving the bachelor party	63.95
Writing thank-you notes	30.38

WINDOW WASHER

Being a window washer	7.7
Washing windows above the 2nd floor	11.445
Washing windows on the outside of a skyscraper, hooked to a harness attached to the building's face	44.62
Washing windows on the outside of a skyscraper, on a scaffold	50.24

WORK

Being asked to share your private office	28.35
The company chairperson discovers a new theory of personnel management	31.46
Your company merges with a company that has a totally different culture	32.83

WORKING

Working in an ad agency	17.65
Working in a factory with a high accident rate	42.67
Working in a nuclear plant	46.234
Working in a cubicle	21.57

WRITING

Writing a business memo	10.45
Writing a business memo, and not knowing how to spell	17.23
Writing a love note	46.87
Writing a Ph.D. dissertation	45.57
Writing a ransom note	43.57
Writing a ransom note, using a lot of different types of letters cut out of newspapers and magazines	20.46
Writing on a computer for the first time	28.573
Being a Luddite and having to use a computer	67.987
Proofreiding a long dockumint	7.24
Knowing that readers look at your work and say, "I could have done that!"	0.032

YOUR CALL CANNOT BE COMPLETED AS DIALED	6.55
YOUR CARD IS UNREADABLE	29.4
YOUR CARD HAS BEEN RETAINED	44.832
YOUR PAPERS, PLEASE	49.33

Appendix #1: The Variability of Stress

While this book provides the most comprehensive stress ratings ever developed, it should be remembered that stress is experienced differently by different individuals, and that stress is not strictly linear in its cumulative properties. A stressor, if it is the only stressor that you are experiencing, generally has greater impact than if it is only one of four stressors you are suffering. Except, of course, when that one of four stressors is the proverbial straw that busts the dromedary's hump, in which case it has greater impact.

To mathematically depict these relationships requires complex algorithms, similar to those the financial world uses to create derivatives. These sorts of calculations generally exceed the power of most personal computers, and don't yield significantly more accurate valuations than the simpler methodology employed in generating this list. Both are, more or less, accurate at the 52% probability level for a margin of error of plus or minus 50 points. In other words, about as predictive as the weather forecasts on the evening news.

We hope to further refine our measurements in the future, with the help of a Macarthur genius grant (hint, hint.) But, meanwhile, we are confident that we have made a giant step forward over the less situational, more limited stress ratings that have been available up to this point.

Appendix #2

We acknowledge the lively academic debate about the stress ratings of death. Some contend that one's own death deserves a very high rating, in the 100 range. Others think that death rates a zero: the meter is off; the battery dead. Unfortunately, the recent spate of near-death experience books has not resolved the issue. Some of those who have bungee jumped to the brink of life report that the transition they started was calming and peaceful; others, however, report that they were "stressed by the light."

Only when this matter is resolved will our editors let us put in ratings for such events as dying by drowning in oatmeal or dying while in Mahwah, New Jersey.

Appendix #3: Personal Stress Thresholds

Part of the massive ambient inaccuracy and nonrepeatability of various stressful situations comes from the fact that one's tolerance for stress is not constant; it shifts over time.

You can get used to almost anything. You can even learn to love stress—love it to the point of possible addiction.

Stress addiction is an increasingly recognized syndrome and is likely to be more frequently diagnosed in the coming years. It is the kind of diagnosis that HMOs hate (they have to pay for treatment) and drug companies love (new disorders mean new overpriced medications).

In stress addiction cases, individuals become so inured to higher stress levels that they only feel good when they are operating under extreme stress. They associate pressure with well-being. These people make great employees, lovers, friends, relatives, coworkers and neighbors, right up to the moment when they snap.

Appendix #4: Signs of Excessive Stress

Excessive stress can manifest itself in a vast number of ways. Here are just a few of the key signs to look for:

- *Sleeping too much*
- *Insomnia*
- *Compulsive overeating*
- *Loss of appetite*
- *Becoming silent and withdrawn*
- *Becoming loud and bombastic*
- *Talking to yourself*
- *Excessive use of profanity*

- *Nonuse of profanity by a Marine*
- *The heartbreak of psoriasis*
- *Steam coming out of ears*
- *Eyes popping*
- *Nail biting*
- *Teeth grinding*
- *Bulging neck muscles*
- *Back pain*
- *Misalignment of chakras*
- *Dingy aura*
- *Lopsided karma*

Appendix #5: Stress Reduction Measures You Can Take

It would seem irresponsible, although hardly surprising, for us to identify so many stressors without mentioning, at least in passing, some of the recognized methods of personal stress reduction. After an exhausting (for us) study of the literature in this area, we have realized that stress reduction methods generally fit into one of the following categories:

The Meditative

The Royal Canadian Mountie meditation program introduced in the 1960s with its motto "We always get our mantra," and all of the meditation-based stress-reduction programs that have followed it, counteract stress by teaching subjects how to enter another state of consciousness. Subjects return to reality relaxed—but the stressors are still present. The meditation is transcendental, but sometimes, unfortunately, the benefits are transitory.

The Athletic

The famous "Fit for Strife" regimen, and the other programs that suggest exercise as a way to combat stress, boast the dual benefits of strengthening the body against the predations of stress, as well as offering a temporary escape from stress when the brain is deprived of oxygen that is being rerouted to overworked muscles. One of the drawbacks of this method is the acute withdrawal symptoms that the exercise-addicted experience on days when they can't exercise. This causes them great stress.

The Confessional

Religious confession, as well as most forms of noninteractive therapy, works on the theory that identifying the stress and trying to pass some of it off onto another human, who may or may not be listening and may or may not care, is salutary. Of course, if you respect the person to whom you are confessing and value his/her opinion, having to admit your errors, foibles and peccadilloes to this person can cause great stress, especially if the person decides to use what you've said against you.

The Empowering

A number of anti-stress regimens and therapies seek to help their adherents focus on specific stressing bugaboos, such as fear of flying or fear that when they are away on business their spouses will have affairs or rearrange the living room furniture. Other therapies, such as assertiveness (stress the first syllable) training, seek to equip the subject to battle a broader range of stresses. Patients learn to stop being doormats and become towers of strength, despised by all the doormats they now dance on.

The Humorous

Ultimately, however, the best stress reduction tool is humor—specifically, repeatedly reading this book. For safety's sake, we generally recommend that you buy one copy for each bathroom in your home and workplace, as well as a "car copy."

To enhance the therapeutic value of this book, share it with others. Buy them copies, or badger them into buying copies. Do not loan yours out, unless you have memorized every entry and rating in the book!!! Once everyone in your circle of friends possesses at least one copy of this book, you can call, fax and e-mail each other and compare cumulative stress totals.

Important Warning

Do not commence a stress reduction program without first consulting a professional. If you are a professional, consult another professional whom you suspect makes more money than you do.

This book is in no way intended to be a substitute for an enlightening relationship with someone who can help craft a personalized program tailored to your particular circumstances and your ability to change, and pay.

Your Stress Diary

The following blank pages are provided so you can note stressors we may have omitted. Be sure to add the appropriate stress value next to your entry. NOTE: Making these notations may well be a stress-reducing activity.

Notes

Notes